About the Autho

Formerly a successful businessman, N.] many years, been teaching just about e' about every sort of pupil in just about ev̲e̲r̲y̲ ̲s̲o̲r̲t̲ ̲o̲f̲ ̲c̲i̲r̲c̲u̲m- stance – English, Latin, Greek, French, German, mathematics, history, classical philosophy, natural medicine, the elements of music and 'How to start up and run your own business' – in lecture halls, large classrooms, small classrooms and homes – to pupils from three years old to over seventy – of many different nationalities and in several different countries – and, since 2007, 'face-to-face' over the Internet.

His teaching methods are very much in accordance with the traditional, common-sense ones, refined over the centuries, that were used almost everywhere until they were abolished worldwide in the 1960s and subsequently.

His teaching has been considered sufficiently remarkable – both in its unusualness today's world and in its genuinely speedy effectiveness – to have featured in a newspaper and in magazine articles and on television and in radio programmes.

Previously published books by him are:

Gwynne's Grammar: The Ultimate Introduction to Grammar and the Writing of Good English. (Ebury Press, London 2013)

Gwynne's Grammar: The Ultimate Introduction to Grammar and the Writing of Good English. (Alfred A. Knopf, New York, 2013) An expanded version of the Ebury Press edition.

Gwynne's Latin: The Ultimate Introduction to Latin Including the Latin in Everyday English. (Ebury Press, London, 2013)

Gwynne's Kings and Queens: The Indispensable History of England and Her Monarchs. (Ebury Press, London, May 2018)

Gwynne's Evolution or Creation? (St. Edward's Press, Swindon, Wilts, July 2020)

The Truth about Rodrigo Borgia, Pope Alexander VI (Lulu.com, July 2008)

Gwynne's
William Shakespeare

At long last, the *reality* – the *demonstrable* reality.

And was Shakespeare
the single most influential person
– whether beneficially influential or otherwise –
in English history?

by N. M. Gwynne, M. A. (Oxon)

St. Edward's Press Ltd.

Formal Notes

Gwynne's William Shakespeare

First published in 2020 by

St. Edward's Press Ltd

20 Barra Close

Highworth

Swindon

Wilts

SN67HX

1st edition

ISBN 978-1-909650-15-2

Cover design by 659design, Highworth
Printed by Ashford Ltd, Gosport.

Contents

Preface.

This book does not aim at completeness in its treatment of the subject, William Shakespeare. Apart from anything else, a vast number of pages would be needed for such an undertaking, and even the task of reading them would be off-puttingly daunting.

What this book *does* aim at is to put before its readers a more satisfactory job in what it sets out to do than, in its totality, has ever been achieved before, and also to do so readably and enjoyably for those who are prepared to work their way through it with open minds.

Against that background, I think that I should next make it clear that I have an expectation that I suppose to be an unusual one in an author who believes his book to be a worthwhile contribution to the world of literature on a subject of undoubted importance. This is that I believe it to be very possible that the reception of this book

> *either* will be hostile,
>
> *or* will even be *very* hostile, and for no genuinely *valid* reason,
>
> *or* will be verging on non-existent.

What, as outlined above, I am foreseeing – rightly or wrongly, and of course I should much prefer wrongly – is despite my thinking:

> in the first place, that there can be few subjects of even *equal* importance to the subject of William Shakespeare, let alone of greater importance,

> and, in the second place, that I can justifiably believe my offering on him (a) to be, as mentioned above, worthwhile, and even valuable; (b) to be one of very few books ever published to take its particular position on the first of its two main topics; and (c) to put in front of its readers a *reality* about William Shakespeare which, although surely a fairly evident reality as soon as it is pointed out, has scarcely ever been offered to the world's reading public before.

I think that there is one other thing worth saying in this preliminary look at what is in this book. This is that, of all the topics outside religious ones that have been subjects for discussion since the dawn of recorded history, the number of which of course verges on infinite, I doubt if there has ever been a more interesting one than the one being addressed here. Again and again, the relevant and *demonstrable* truth that will be emerging in these pages is not merely improbable but often – and in the highest degree – even startling.

And if, good reader, you should think that I must surely be exaggerating – exaggerating at least a little and possibly more than a little – in what I have just said, please keep it in mind and see if you still hold that view as you come to the last page of this book.

*   *   *   *   *

As in the case of all my books published in recent years, readers who have any queries to put, corrections to suggest, or criticisms to offer are welcome to contact me, and indeed even urged to do so in the case anything important falling under any of those three headings.

N. M. Gwynne.

nmg@nmgwynne.com

www.gwynneteaching.com

PART I
The plays of William Shakespeare:
deeply controversial in their content.

Chapter 1

Introductory.

The influence of the author of the plays that are – I am wording this carefully – *attributed* to William Shakespeare, whom, for the time being, I shall continue to refer to by that name for practical convenience even though the identity of the author has been much disputed over the centuries, is an influence that has never been even approached by any other literary figure in any country. It is an influence, moreover,

(a) that has not been limited to England, where of course the author lived and wrote, but has extended worldwide, and

(b) has done so during a period that has so far lasted for more than four hundred years.

This influence, moreover, has almost certainly been greater by far than the influence exercised by any other single person during those centuries, not excluding the best-known politicians and philosophers of the era.

Lest it be thought by some readers to be at least a possibility that I have exaggerated in saying that, I offer as support this, in its essence far from untypical introduction to the subject, which I have taken from a useful booklet, *Was Shakespeare Educated?*, by W. C. C. Gundry (Lapworth & Co. Ltd., 1946):

Foremost of the many great names found in the realm of literature stands the world-famous name *Shakespeare*. By the general sense of civilised nations, Shakespeare's works are placed in a higher category than any other, ancient or modern. Although this outstanding genius is England's son, he is now looked upon as belonging not only to one country but to all mankind. The Shakespeare plays are translated into every important language, and each succeeding year sees an increase in the number of editions.

The literature inspired by Shakespeare's dramatic works is enormous, ranging from the critical writings of Coleridge,

Hazlitt, Schlegel, Lessing, Goethe, Gervinus, Ulrici, Heine, Guizot, Victor Hugo, to hundreds of less known writers.

Whole galleries of paintings by eminent artists, such as Holman Hunt, Millais, Maclise, Landseer, Corot, Delacroix, Fuseli and Retsch reflect his art.

His influence on music has been quite as striking.

To *Romeo and Juliet* we owe Tchaikovsky's concert overture of that name. To *Macbeth* we owe the music of Bantock and Mathew Locke and the tone-poem by Strauss, and also Greig's *Watchman's Song,* which was inspired by witnessing a performance of that play.

To these we must add Sir Edward German's tone-poem *Hamlet* and Sir Edward Elgar's *Falstaff* study; Beethoven's Pianoforte Sonata in F Minor (Opus 57) where the atmosphere of *The Tempest is* suggested; and also Mendelssohn's *Overture To A Midsummer Night's Dream.*

*   *   *   *   *

The extraordinary influence of William Shakespeare can be further considered under five separate headings.

First heading:

Shakespeare's effect on the English language in terms of its vocabulary.

It is not possible to say for certain how many words Shakespeare added to the English language, but it is certainly very many. Max Müller, a highly respected German philologist (philology is the science of language with special reference to its history and to word-comparisons) who spent most of his life in England, in volume I (page 378), published in 1899, of his *Science of Language* estimated Shakespeare's vocabulary at fifteen thousand words, truly astonishing against the background, given by Müller at the same time, that the writer with the *next* biggest English vocabulary, John Milton, was, he estimated, "only" eight thousand words, while a university-educated English person's vocabulary is between three and four thousand words and the average *non*-university-educated person's vocabulary is less than a thousand words.

Indeed Shakespeare's is the single greatest contribution to the status of the English language (a) in its possession of the largest vocabulary of any language today and (b) in its being the richest and most expressive language that has ever existed.

We can get some idea of what English owes to him simply by listing, in alphabetical order, some of the words he invented that begin with the first letter of the English alphabet:

abstemious, academe, accessible, accommodation, accused, addiction, admirable, aerial, airless, alligator, amazement, anchovy, arch-villain, arouse, assassination, auspicious.

All those words starting with the letter "a" owe their origin to Shakespeare, and there may be more.

Starting with the letter b:

backing, bandit, barefaced, beached, bedroom, besmirch, bet, birthplace, bloodstained, bump, buzzer.

And so on, through the alphabet.

Second heading:

Shakespeare's effect on the English language in terms of common English expressions.

This aspect of Shakespeare's output is of great importance not least because language governs the thinking and thoughts of us human beings to quite a considerable extent, from which it follows that, if it be the case that the effect of Shakespeare's writings on the English *language* has been considerable, so, too, must his effect on the *thinking* of all English-speaking people have been considerable.

Certainly his effect on the English language has been vast. Several pages could be devoted to showing this but probably sufficient for practical purposes is the following wonderfully well-put-together summary of just one single feature of his writings by a leading journalist of his day, the late Bernard Levin. It originally appeared as part of an article published in the London *Times* newspaper a few decades ago and was subsequently reproduced in a book by Levin published in 1970, *The Pendulum Years: Britain in the Sixties.*

If you cannot understand my argument, and declare "It's Greek to me", you are quoting Shakespeare.

If you claim to be more sinned against than sinning, you are quoting Shakespeare.

If you recall your salad days, you are quoting Shakespeare.

If you act more in sorrow than in anger, if your wish is father to the thought, and if your lost property has vanished into thin air, you are quoting Shakespeare.

If you have ever refused to budge an inch or suffered from green-eyed jealousy, if you have played fast and loose, if you have been tongue-tied, a tower of strength, hoodwinked or in a pickle, if you have knitted your brows, made a virtue of necessity, insisted on fair play, slept not one wink, stood on ceremony, danced attendance (on your lord and master), laughed yourself into stitches, had short shrift or cold comfort or too much of a good thing, if you have seen better days or lived in a fool's paradise – why, be that as it may, the more fool you, for it is a foregone conclusion that you are (as good luck would have it) quoting Shakespeare.

If you think it is early days and you clear out bag and baggage, if you think it is high time and that is the long and short of it, if you believe that the game is up and that truth will out even if it involves your own flesh and blood, if you lie low till the crack of doom because you suspect foul play, if, at one fell swoop, you have your teeth set on edge without rhyme or reason, then – to give the devil his due – if the truth were known, you are, if you have a tongue in your head, quoting Shakespeare.

Even if you bid me good riddance and send me packing, if you wish I was dead as a door-nail, if you think I am an eyesore, a laughing stock, the devil incarnate, a stony-hearted villain, bloody-minded or a blinkin' idiot, then – by Jove! O Lord! Tut, tut! for goodness' sake! what the dickens! but me no buts – it is all one to me,... for you are quoting Shakespeare.

I believe my readers would do well to read that passage at least one more time before proceeding further in these pages. It is difficult to come anywhere near to grasping the extent of Shakespeare's contribution to our language until it has, so to speak, become soaked into our brains.

Third heading:

Other than the authors collectively put together in the Bible, Shakespeare is by far the most widely-read writer today, and not only in England but worldwide.

Other authors have gained renown and reverence outside as well as inside their native countries, and have been translated into languages other than their authors' native languages. Obvious examples are Dante of Italy; Racine, Corneille, Rousseau and Voltaire of France; Goethe and Schiller of Germany; Tolstoy and Dostoevsky of Russia. Shakespeare is unique, however, in having become part of even the *culture* of other countries, the most extreme example being the United States, the very capital of which, Washington D.C., honours him *with a whole museum*, the Folger Library, dedicated to him at the very centre of that city, next door to the Library of Congress and very close to the White House.

Fourth heading:

Shakespeare is by a very long way the most-performed playwright that has ever existed.

On any day of the year there is a Shakespeare performance in all of the world's major cities, even as far away as India and Japan, and in many of the world's lesser cities as well. In addition, well over four hundred film versions of his plays have been produced so far, *many* more than of any other author.

Fifth and final heading:

Shakespeare is even expressly honoured by a whole town.

Yes, the town Stratford-upon-Avon in Warwickshire has for some time been dedicated to revering and promoting Shakespeare. Indeed he is even honoured by a whole *county*: road-signs at each of the county boundaries crossing into Warwickshire – those of Gloucestershire, Leicestershire, Oxfordshire, Northampton-shire, Staffordshire, Worcestershire and the West – specify "Shakes-peare's County". No English monarch or war-leader has come within even a remote distance of being honoured in such a way, let alone any other "mere" writer.

Do any of my readers wonder if what I have being claiming, as to the uniquely immense status and influence of William Shake-speare in the world today, is perhaps a little exaggerated, or even *more* than a little exaggerated? Those of you, if there are any, who do can safely cast such doubt from your mind. If anything, I have been understating.

Is that difficult to believe? Here, to more than back me up – please excuse that split infinitive – is as solid an authority as anyone could ask for: the Artistic Director of Stratford-on Avon's Royal Shakespeare Company, recipient of the Hay Festival Medal for Drama, and a respected author on things Shakespearean, Mr. Gregory Doran – referred to in the *Sunday Times* newspaper as "one of the great Shakespeareans of his generation". Writing in the London *Daily Telegraph* of 23rd April 2020:

Dear Shakespeare,

I am sorry we have had to cancel your birthday this year. Normally on the Saturday nearest to April 23, the streets of Stratford-upon-Avon are lined with crowds. Dignitaries process, bands parade, flags are unfurled, balloons are released and glitter cannons fired.

There are lectures and sermons and awards and ceremonial dinners and lunches in your honour. Cakes are cut, wreaths are laid, and hats are worn. A quill is held aloft by the head boy of your old school and placed in the hand of your funerary monument in Holy Trinity Church. And, of course, there is a special birthday performance by the Royal Shakespeare Company, of which I am proud to be the artistic director. It would have been *The Winter's Tale* this year...

There is an entire industry around your work. I just typed your name into Google, which shows 242million results in 0.77 seconds.

All this about an *author*? No, I have indeed not been exaggerating. In fact when it comes to Shakespeare, again and again exaggeration seems to be impossible.

Well, is it for better or for worse that William Shakespeare has been enjoying, and is still enjoying, this extraordinary reverence and influence? Certainly we ought to *hope* that it is for the better, since everyone in the English-speaking world, typically starting from childhood, is affected by him, as indeed are countless people in the rest of the world. Whether it is or is not is clearly a subject well worth exploring.

*   *   *   *   *

So far, in what I have been offering, there has, I think, been nothing to raise any hackles. So far, but no longer... Disappointingly, this period of literary tranquility is now about to come to an end.

"*Audi alteram partem*" – "Hear the other side."

Against the background of much experience over many years, I can safely say that, however regrettably, seldom, if ever, do those words just quoted need to be more emphatically uttered. In this case they are directed at dedicated admirers and lovers of the works of the Bard of Avon, and of course also to authors on any of the many subjects relating to those works.

This is what I now say to such readers, hoping that they will not find it impertinent, or objectionable in any other respect.

Please, all of you, remember that is our constant duty – the duty of you, me and everyone – to make *honest use* of our reason and *not* to *betray* our reason.

That is to say, it is our duty to be guided in our judgements *strictly* by relevant arguments and evidence, and irrespective of what our emotions and feelings may be on any subject. This is because our emotions – as traditional philosophy insists – are *not* for *making judgements* as to what is, for instance, true and beautiful in any area that we can have experience of. Rather, our emotions are for loving those things that combine truth and beauty, and that are *therefore* worthy of our love, *after* we have identified them as such *with our reason*.

Please, therefore, good readers, set aside any prejudices as you read on. Please, too, be prepared to gulp at what is immediately to come!

*   *   *   *   *

I now, daringly, take it upon myself to state that it is demonstrable, even readily demonstrable:

(a) that the works attributed to Shakespeare are the single greatest literary influence for evil that has existed in the last thousand years and more, and

(b) that the most objectively suitable treatment for those works, notwithstanding the general desirability of free speech, would be to make it actually illegal even to *read* them, let alone to perform and to see them performed.

This is not to suggest or imply that Shakespeare did not have an important and beneficial influence on the English language. As we saw earlier in this chapter, Shakespeare's is the single greatest contribution to the English language's vocabulary being the largest vocabulary of any language today and of the English language being the richest and most expressive language in all history. No, I am making reference to the *content* of the works of Shakespeare, not the *manner* in which the content is presented, which indeed is compelling in the highest degree, and in consequence making it all the more dangerous to the average reader. Hence my belief that, ideally, the works of Shakespeare would be subjected to censorship, and I mean *heavy* censorship.

Such censorship would not be a practical policy, of course; but I do not hesitate to assert that the world would be a better place if it could be imposed.

*   *   *   *   *

How can such a claim, in effect that Shakespeare is potentially pernicious in his effects on those exposed to his works – contrary to the esteem that is accorded to Shakespeare as it is – be worth making, let alone worth inviting readers to take seriously?

As I have just indicated, what I shall certainly *not* be doing in what follows is disputing the beauty of Shakespeare's *language*. Far from it. On the contrary, it is my firm belief that it this very feature of his output, this beauty of the language in which it is expressed, that seduces people into allowing themselves to be blinded to the reality of Shakespeare, even though that reality can become completely obvious if we are prepared to open our minds and, so to speak, mentally blink so that the scales fall from our eyes.

The possibility of beauty being used destructively to promote what is evil was wonderfully well highlighted by the 18th century United States Congressman John Randolph of Roanoke, a famous orator of his day, when referring to a fellow-politician in the eighteenth century:

Like rotten mackerel by moonlight, he shines and he stinks.

Yes, I am fully entitled to ask you, gracious readers, indeed to plead with you, not to allow the beauty of the language in which the works of Shakespeare are written to be anything approaching a deciding factor when assessing those works. That is to say, I ask you not to be so dazzled by *how* he says what he says as to fail to look closely enough into exactly *what it is* that he is saying.

*   *   *   *   *

Before I address the sad reality about William Shakespeare, however, and bending over backwards to be completely fair to him before I proceed to take him to pieces, I am going to invite readers to enjoy just one example of him at his very best, showing what wonderful works of literature and art his plays *could* have been if he had used his intelligence and talents as we must wish he had, rather than as he did.

Many readers will already be aware of the piece of verse that now follows, and some will know it well. It was indeed once justly described, by David Marquand in the monthly periodical *The Literary Review* of December 1990, as "the most memorable expression of English nationalism ever written."

From *King Richard the Second*, Act II, Scene 1, and declaimed by John of Gaunt:

> This royal throne of kings, this sceptered isle,
> This earth of majesty, this seat of Mars,
> This other Eden, demi-paradise,
> This fortress built by Nature for herself
> Against infection and the hand of war,
> This happy breed of men, this little world,
> This precious stone set in the silver sea,
> Which serves it in the office of a wall
> Or as a moat defensive to a house,
> Against the envy of less happier lands –
> This blessed plot, this earth, this realm, this England.

$$*\qquad*\qquad*\qquad*\qquad*$$

Finally, worth including, to round off our opening look at the phenomenon that is Shakespeare, is this extract from a review in the *Daily Mail* (8th October 2020) of a recently-published book *Shakespearean: On Life And Language In Times Of Disruption* by Robert McCrum (Picador, London. 2020):

> In the 17th century, homesick colonists in America read Shakespeare's Complete Works almost as avidly as they read the Holy Bible, finding "a wistful mix of consolation and souvenir".
>
> Shakespeare became an American passion, with Othello often staged in the South before the Civil War and many young black men in the slave states being named Othello.
>
> Meanwhile, at home Shakespeare became such a part of "the national conversation" that a character in Jane Austen's *Mansfield Park* observes: "We all talk Shakespeare."

"Part of the national conversation", and even mentioned in the same breath, so to speak, as the Holy Bible! My readers, we can

justifiably rub our eyes in wonderment at this phenomenon that is
William Shakespeare.

Chapter 2
Is the play *King Henry the Fifth*
worthy of the acclaim that it enjoys?

To open up our search for the reality of Shakespeare's output, let us now plunge into one of his plays.

So that I cannot reasonably be accused of "loading the dice" by carefully selecting a play *simply* because I know it to contain material which backs up with unusual force the case that I am about to make, I propose to start with one of the best known and most widely admired of his plays, *King Henry the Fifth.*

In order that we may be soundly placed to make a satisfactory judgement of this play, what we need to do first of all is to acquaint ourselves adequately with the *reality* of this English king in his actual life and reign. I can safely offer as trustworthy what I shall now put forward for this purpose because the information in it comes from the chapter devoted to him in my book *Gwynne's Kings and Queens*! – for which extensive and careful research was needed, as anyone who is acquainted with the usual, and very different, presentation of King Henry V and his reign will appreciate.

How it is that I can be confident that what now follows is in fact trustworthy, even though in conflict, as indeed it is, with that presented by most other English historians who give King Henry V their attention, will, I think, become obvious enough as we proceed.

$$* \qquad * \qquad * \qquad * \qquad *$$

Soon after succeeding his father, King Henry IV, to the throne in 1413, King Henry V launched an attempt to win back the territories in France that had been lost by his ancestors in the relatively recent past. This amounted to a resumption of what is known as The Hundred Years' War, which had started in 1337 and come to a temporary end nearly five decades later, in 1381.

After overcoming various difficulties, King Henry achieved a great victory at the battle subsequently made famous throughout the entire world by Shakespeare, the three-hour Battle of Agincourt, Agincourt being a small village in the north-east of France. Thanks to the skill of the English archers with the longbow, no fewer than twenty thousand French soldiers were defeated by a mere six thousand English soldiers.

Subsequent campaigns, in 1417 and 1419, were also eventually successful; and King Henry ended up being, although not until long after his death, England's most glorified king since the Norman Conquest, and second only to King Alfred the Great in the popular estimation of his worth.

Some historians, indeed, might even put him above King Alfred the Great. For a useful summary of what is generally thought of him, here is a relatively recent historian, Desmond Seward, in the Introduction in his book *Henry V as Warlord*, published by Sidgwick & Jackson in 1987:

> Henry V is one of England's heroes. The victor of Agincourt was idolised during his lifetime; his memory inspired one of Shakespeare's most stirring plays; and the Victorians considered him a perfect Christian gentleman. "He was religious, pure in life, temperate, liberal, careful and yet splendid," says Bishop Stubbs in chapter XVIII of the third volume of his *The Constitutional History of England*, published in 1878; "merciful, truthful and honourable, discreet in word, provident in counsel, prudent in judgement, modest in look, magnanimous in act, a true Englishman."
>
> That brilliant historian of the mediaeval English, the late K. B. McFarlane, thought Henry "the greatest man that ever ruled England".

But no, that great reverence was not even remotely justifiable. Proceeding, in that book's same Introduction, a little further with Desmond Seward, who is the only English historian, as far as I know, to have taken a significantly different position from that one:

> Nevertheless, his conquest of France was as much about loot as dynastic succession, accompanied by mass slaughter,

arson and rape. After it, French plunder was on sale all over England...

The misery inflicted on the French by Henry's campaigns is indisputable. Any local historian in north-western France can point to a town, a chateau, an abbey or a church sacked by his men. When the English raided enemy territory, they killed anything that moved, destroyed crops and food supplies and drove off livestock...

Occupied areas fared little better because of the *pâtis,* or protection racket, operated by English garrisons; villages had to pay extortionate dues in food and wine as well as money, failure to deliver sometimes incurred executions and burnings.

Yes, gracious readers: mass slaughter, arson and rape. To any of you who may suppose that to be typical of how warfare was conducted in the Middle Ages, I say emphatically: no, that is not so. It was not, for instance, how Kings Edward I and III fought in France during their endless campaigns. Nor has any such conduct been suggested even of supposedly "Bad" King John.

Indeed, I doubt that there is a single precedent in Christian warfare for Henry's methods. Nor was anything resembling what Desmond Seward has just outlined to be repeated until some centuries later.

The reality is that arguably the most astonishing of all the achievements of the Catholic Church, after England's conversion to Christianity by St. Augustine of Canterbury at the end of the sixth century A.D., was its success in *civilising* warfare. Considering war to be a great evil, but also realistically recognising that it was inevitable in a world that would always contain sinners as well as saints, the Church did what it could to mitigate its disastrous effects and to reduce its evils to the minimum that was practically possible; and it achieved that throughout Europe to an extent that is unimaginable today.

Mass slaughter, arson and rape. The reality is that the supposedly "perfect Christian gentleman" who was "the greatest man that ever ruled England" appears to have been a man who was immoral, nasty and despicable in his conduct of warfare.

Then whence comes the very different depiction of his that is almost universal? Granted, King Henry V was regarded as something of paragon among kings by earlier English writers, but the extremeness of the glamorous picture of him and of his glorification that has been part of English culture of the last half a dozen centuries we owe *primarily* to Shakespeare.

*   *   *   *   *

Our first look at Shakespeare's treatment of history, and the exposure of him as a gross falsifier of historical reality, has not been encouraging. It must be reasonable to wonder whether that is an isolated instance of such falsification or an example that is all too typical of his output.

It must be worth wondering too, now that he has been shown to be unreliable in his glorifying representation of an important public figure, whether he is *also* guilty of the *opposite* form of historical perversion. That is to say, whether, in addition, Shakespeare is guilty of traducing the *good* name of a virtuous king.

We must hope not, for such would be an even worse moral crime than that of promoting a war-criminal as a man of virtue. Traditional Christian teaching holds calumny, the malicious depiction of a good person as the opposite, to be one of the gravest of all moral crimes, and of course all the graver, the greater the misrepresentation.

Perhaps the most obvious place to go first, in our quest for an example of the opposite kind of misrepresentation, *if* any should exist (which, as just mentioned, we must *hope* is not the case), is his depiction of England's king who is the most apparently evil of them all. To King Richard the Third, in the Shakespeare play named after him, we shall therefore now turn.

Chapter 3
The play *King Richard the Third*.

At the beginning of the period of history featured by Shakespeare in his play *King Richard the Third*, the so-called Wars of the Roses of 1455 to 1487 – a civil war between two rival families for the throne of England, the House of Lancaster and the House of York – had just come to an end. The House of York had been victorious, and, under King Edward IV of the House of York, England was at last enjoying a period of peace.

According to Shakespeare, the general rejoicing that resulted was, however, by no means shared by King Edward IV's physically deformed younger brother, Richard, Duke of Gloucester. Very much to the contrary: Richard bitterly resented both the power that now belonged to King Edward and the happiness of those who had supported him. Power-hungry, malicious, and embittered by having to live with his physical appearance, Richard at once set his heart on gaining the throne for himself, and, as he embarked on this quest, he took the ruthless decision to use any means of deception and of political manipulation that he might find necessary in his pursuit of the kingship, and even to engage in mass-murder if that should seem necessary.

Swiftly putting his plan into action, he first of all manoeuvred a noblewoman, Lady Anne Nevill, into marrying him, succeeding in getting her agreement to this even though – as, according to Shakespeare, she was well aware – he had murdered her first husband. He then committed an act of judicial murder, in having one of his two elder brothers, the Duke of Clarence, executed, which he was able to organise because his eldest brother King Edward had become gravely ill and practically speaking was no longer ruling. Finally, he accelerated the death of King Edward himself by successfully shifting onto him the burden of guilt for the murder of their brother Clarence that he himself had perpetrated, and, thereby causing a worsening of King Edward's illness.

King Edward IV's death did not result in Richard coming immediately to the throne, because the throne was automatically inherited by the eldest of Edward's two young sons, also Edward by name. In accordance with the late King Edward's stated wish, however, Richard became officially the Lord Protector, and thus in reality the ruler of England during the young Edward's minority. He would legitimately remain in that office until Edward, formerly the Prince of Wales and now King Edward V, reached the age of adulthood, when he could *rule* as king as well as *reign* as king.

Once established as Lord Protector, Richard set about eliminating – by bringing about their death – those of the court noblemen who were loyal to the young princes, most notably Lord Hastings, the Lord Chamberlain of England. He then proceeded to have arrested and executed all the most powerful relations of the two boys' mother, the now-widowed Queen Elizabeth, with the result that Queen Elizabeth herself and her two sons, the young King Edward V and his younger brother, Richard, Duke of York, were then all of them unprotected.

Richard's next step was to set about organising his political allies into a campaign to have himself, Richard, crowned. In this he was successful.

Once king, one of his first actions was to commit the two young princes to imprisonment in the Tower of London. Shortly afterwards, he organised their murder.

By now, Richard's reign of terror had caused the common people of England to fear and loathe him, and he had also alienated nearly all the noblemen of the court.

Various rumours then began to circulate. One was that the Earl of Richmond – a member of the Lancaster family that had lost the civil war, the Wars of the Roses, from which the Yorks had emerged victorious – was about to make a challenge for the throne and was gathering forces in France. Another was that many of England's noblemen were abandoning King Richard to join Richmond's forces. Yet another was that they and the populace in England as a generality were fully ready to welcome the Earl of Richmond.

None of this deterred Richard from continuing his ruthless consolidation of his power. His next victim was his own wife, Queen Anne, whom he murdered so that he could marry his young niece Elizabeth, she being the daughter of his brother – the dead King Edward IV – and of King Edward's wife Queen Elizabeth. His motive for the murder was to create an alliance that would keep his claim to the throne secure.

At this point Richard at last began to lose control of events. In particular, his brother's widow, the former Queen Elizabeth, succeeded in forestalling him, secretly promising to marry off her young daughter Elizabeth to the Earl of Richmond if this were to become possible.

Now at last the Earl of Richmond invaded England, and there followed a famous battle, the Battle of Bosworth.

The night before this battle, which would finally decide everything, King Richard had a terrible dream. The ghosts of all the people whom he had murdered appeared in front of him and cursed him, and told him that he would die on the following day.

In the battle that then took place, King Richard was indeed killed, and the Earl of Richmond was crowned King Henry VII; and, promising a new era of peace for England, the new king was then betrothed to young Elizabeth in order to unite the warring Houses of Lancaster and York.

*   *   *   *   *

"I am determined to prove a villain," says King Richard the Third in his opening speech, the very first speech in the play, in Act I, Scene 1.

And, during the course of what followed in the play, prove a villain he certainly did.

   – He murdered King Henry VI and Edward of Lancaster.

– He contrived the death of his own brother the Duke of Clarence.

– He killed Lord Hastings.

– He arranged the murder of his two child nephews in the Tower of London.

– He poisoned his own wife in order to marry his niece.

– And so on. The number of murders and other killings that feature in the play is so great that it would actually be quite a demanding task even to try to count them, let alone to go on to describe them in any detail.

Should we perhaps, even so, hesitate before assigning great blame to King Richard? After all, as we also learn from the play, he was the victim of terrible circumstances in relation to his birth, which took place after he had spent *two years* in his mother's womb and had then emerged with a complete set of teeth, hair down to his shoulders, a withered arm, a humpback, and one shoulder higher than the other. Can any of us safely say that, if *we* had suffered similar misfortunes when making our entry into this world, that would not have had adverse effects on *our* character?

*　　*　　*　　*　　*

If only because of having been put on general enquiry by what we have learnt from Shakespeare's treatment of King Henry V, it is as well that we now put the question: but *how true* is the story of King Richard III thus presented by William Shakespeare?

The answer?

Although the Shakespeare play, at least in outline, has tended to receive the approval of historians, there is overwhelming evidence that there is scarcely a word of truth in it. I repeat and stress: *scarcely a word.*

Let us start with King Richard's appearance.

There is no definite evidence that King Richard was in any way deformed or otherwise strange in his looks. There are no *contemporary* references to any physical deformities, and no indications of such deformities in the earliest-known portraits of him. Indeed, according to the Right Hon. T. P. Courtney, a highly respected early-nineteenth-century author who was also a Member of Parliament, it was maintained by an elderly friend of his, the Countess of Desmond, who as a young girl danced at the court of his brother Edward IV, that Richard was "the handsomest man in the room except his brother Edward, and…" – note this – "…*was very well made.*" (Italics added.)

Please stare at those words, good readers.

Closer to home, those who would have seen King Richard III as he was included the contemporary author of a publication known as *The Croyland Chronicle*, a historical record that the Benedictine Abbey of Croyland, in Lincolnshire, had started in the early Middle Ages and kept constantly up to date. The chronicler, although having no qualms about making *other* accusations about Richard, makes no reference to any physical peculiarities. Nor do any other contemporary writers.

As to King Richard's character and also the most important things that he is expressly accused of, some examples of the *reality* are:

– He was trusted by his brother King Edward, and was respected and popular in the part of Britain that Edward had delegated to him to administer.

– There is neither any evidence nor any likelihood that Richard murdered King Henry VI.

– It was *not* on his own initiative that he came to the throne in place of his nephew, the young King Edward V. Very much to the contrary, all the indications are that he was as trustworthy a man of his word as anyone who ever lived, which was why his brother Edward was happy to appoint him as Lord Protector of his son, young Edward, if the young Edward should become King before he was of an age when he could rule as well as reign.

What in fact happened was that, after Prince Richard, the Duke of Gloucester, as the future King Richard then was, had taken the traditional oath of allegiance to King Edward V, as his young nephew had just become, Bishop Stillington, who had been a witness of what he now reported, gave testimony that King Edward's father, King Edward IV, had entered into a contract to marry Lady Elizabeth Butler *before* his marriage to Elizabeth Woodville. Under the matrimonial law at that time, this meant (a) that the marriage to Elizabeth Woodville was invalid and therefore (b) that the young King Edward V was of illegitimate birth.

In accordance with its duty once there was serious doubt about Edward's legitimacy, Parliament gave its full agreement to the implications of what Bishop Stillington had revealed, and Prince Richard, Duke of Gloucester, became King Richard. The coronation that then took place was one of the most magnificent ever put on record, with virtually the entire peerage being present and confirming the coronation's undoubted legitimacy.

As to the two princes in the Tower of London, which in those days was not a prison but one of the royal residences, they were much more of a threat to the position of King Richard's *successor*, King Henry VII, than they had ever been to King Richard; and King Henry VII, the first Tudor monarch, certainly did not lack the degree of ruthlessness that the murder would have needed. This is how Josephine Tey, in her novel *The Daughter of Time*, written by her for the *express* purpose of restoring to King Richard III the reputation that he deserved, wraps this matter up.

First, she quotes a typical historian who deals with the period:

It was the settled and considered policy of the Tudors to rid themselves of all rivals to the throne, more especially those heirs of York who remained alive on the accession of Henry VII. In this they were successful, although it was left to Henry VIII to get rid of the last of them.

Then she gives the reaction to those words of her fictional police-detective, Inspector Alan Grant, who is the hero in her novel:

He stared at this bald announcement. This placid acceptance of wholesale murder. The simple acknowledgement of a process of family elimination.

Richard III had been credited with the elimination of two nephews, and his name was a synonym for evil. But Henry VII, whose "settled and considered policy" was to eliminate *a whole family*, was regarded as a shrewd and far-seeing monarch. Not very lovable perhaps, but constructive and painstaking, and very successful withal.

Grant gave up. History was something that he would never understand. The values of historians differed so *radically* from any values with which he was acquainted that he could never hope to meet them on any common ground. He would have to go back to the Yard [Scotland Yard], where murderers were murderers and what went for Cox went equally for Box.

*   *   *   *   *

It is worth mentioning – if only because, if I do not, others may do so in order to discredit the account given above – the two nearest-to-being-contemporary pieces of writing that support Shakespeare.

The earlier of them is *The History of King Richard III* attributed to – I chose those last two words deliberately – Sir Thomas More, a greatly venerated political figure of King Henry VIII's reign and in due course to be officially canonised as a saint. Born in 1478 and dying in 1535, his life just overlapped with King Richard III, who, as we learnt earlier, died in the battlefield in the Battle of Bosworth. Although he at one time served King Henry VIII as Lord Chancellor, Sir Thomas ended up being, on King Henry's orders, executed for treason when he refused to acknowledge the King Henry as "Supreme Head of the Church of England" when the King took it upon himself:

(a) to separate England from the Catholic Church,

(b) and, breaking new theological ground, to take the Pope's place by putting himself in complete charge of the Church in England even though he was only a layman.

The History of King Richard III attributed to Sir Thomas More certainly supports Shakespeare's position on King Richard III, very much so. Here is some of what is said in its opening pages:

Richard, the third son of the then Duke of York, who, of Royal blood, for a few years governed England as Lord Protector when the then-King, Henry VI, went through a period of insanity, was in intelligence and courage equal with either of them.

In body and prowess, however, he was beneath them – he was little of stature, ill-featured of limbs, crook-backed, with his left shoulder much higher than his right shoulder, and unpleasant to look at. He was malicious, wrathful, envious and perverse. It is credibly reported that the Duchess his mother had much ado when giving birth to him and that he came into the world with the feet forward, *and*, rumour has it, with a full set of teeth.

He was by no means a bad leader in war, which was more suited to his character than was peacetime

He was close and secret, a deep deceiver, lowly of countenance, arrogant of heart, and cruel, not so much out of bad will as, rather, from ambition. For him, friend and foe were according to where he saw his advantage, and he spared no man whose life was to his disadvantage With his own hands, he slew King Henry the Sixth, when that King was a prisoner in the Tower of London

Well, yes. How safe, though, is it to trust what *The History of King Richard III* has just been telling us?

To a reasonably critical eye, it does not come within a million miles – if I may be pardoned for that tiny exaggeration! – of being safe. For instance:

In the first place, Sir Thomas More never made any claim to be that book's author.

In the second place, it was not published until some time after Sir Thomas More's death.

In the third place, it was not written in the scholarly style that Sir Thomas's many other writings would lead us to expect from him, and indeed its manner of composition is very much more "dramatic" than is to be expected of mediaeval chronicles.

In the fourth place – and on the face of it strangely – after Sir Thomas's death two copies of the book were found, one written in English and the other, probably a translation of the former, in Latin.

All that, and especially the last of those facts, has led many people to doubt that Sir Thomas was in fact the author. For instance, Sir Clements Markham, a notable scholar of the 19th century, and, amongst other important academic positions that he held, President of the Royal Geographical Society, thought that the actual author was probably Cardinal John Morton, Archbishop of Canterbury and Lord Chancellor of England and that Morton might have given it to Sir Thomas to translate.

In my opinion the notion that Cardinal Morton was the real author is very credible.

Certainly, as is generally recognised by historians, he was very much a foe of the Yorkist regime in general and of King Richard III in particular, so much so that King Richard at one point went so far as to have him imprisoned. Certainly, too, he was a strong supporter of King Henry VII's very tenuous claim to the throne, and indeed only a few months after King Henry's accession to the throne in 1485 the King, perhaps in recognition of Cardinal Morton's loyalty, organised that he should be appointed Archbishop of Canterbury, and, a year later, made him Lord Chancellor of England.

That appointment, incidentally, was momentous in one of its results. As Lord Chancellor, Morton went so far as to be responsible for the introduction of a new phrase into the English language which made him lastingly famous, when he invented and implemented the scandalously unscrupulous "Morton's Fork" system of taxation, in which, in the words of Morton himself:

If the subject is seen to live frugally, tell him that, because he is clearly a money-saver of great ability, he can afford to give generously to the King. If, however, the subject lives a life of great extravagance, tell him that he, too, can afford to give largely, the proof of his opulence being evident in his expenditure.

(The dictionary-definition of "Morton's Fork" is "a dilemma in which both choices are equally undesirable".)

By contrast with Morton, Sir Thomas More was unable to enjoy a lasting friendship with the monarch of his time. His relationship with King Henry VIII very much *started* as one of friendship, when he first became secretary and personal adviser to the King and then, as mentioned above, Lord Chancellor. When, however, King Henry took the extraordinary and completely unprecedented step of making himself head of the Christian Church in England – which was actually absurd, given that he was only a layman – Sir Thomas found himself unable to accept this, and therefore refused to sign the so-called Oath of Supremacy and other documents that would have involved his acknowledging the King's spiritual supremacy in England, for which there was no possible logical justification.

In 1534 the Treason Act was passed, declaring that to oppose the King's spiritual supremacy was treason. It was held, moreover, that opposing the King's spiritual supremacy included a person even simply keeping silent on the matter if challenged, and the Act had the eventual result that More was beheaded on 6th July 1535.

The upshot: it must be much more likely that Cardinal Morton was the author of *The History of King Richard III* than that Sir Thomas More was, and it is far from improbable that this book is primarily responsible for the grossly false picture of King Richard

III that Josephine Tey exposes as such in her informative novel *The Daughter of Time*.

After Sir Thomas More's book, the next source, chronologically, to be in substantial agreement with Shakespeare's position on King Richard III is *Hollinshed's Chronicles of England, Scotland and Ireland*, a multi-volume collection of historical records and facts of which two slightly different editions were published, one in 1577 and one in 1587. *Hollinshed's*, however, makes it expressly clear in its contents page that what it says about King Richard III comes directly from the *The History of King Richard III* attributed to Sir Thomas More. These are the relevant words in the contents page:

> The Historie of King Edward the Fifth, and King Richard the Third unfinished, written by maister Thomas More then one of the under shiriffes of London, about the yeare of our Lord 1513, according to a copie of his owne hand, printed among his other workes.

Against the first word of the first sentence of the opening paragraph of that chapter of *Hollinshed's*, there is an asterisk, which is one of a number of asterisks referring to notes in the margin. The first of the marginal notes thus referred to says this:

> What is here between this mark [the asterisk] and the next mark was not written by Master More in this *Historie* written by him in English but is translated out of this *Historie* which he wrote in Latin.

Then, a few lines later there are two asterisks, one at the beginning of a sentence and the other at the end of the same sentence, and these refer to this margin-note:

> From this asterisk to the next is not found in Thomas More's *Historie* but in the *Historie* of Hall and Grignon.

That, of course, leaves no room for any doubt that the *rest* of what is quoted on this subject in *Hollinshed's* output is taken from the book attributed to Sir Thomas More. The reality, therefore, is, in the first place, that Shakespeare's horrifyingly false picture of King Richard III is that *of a single writer*, the one widely supposed to be Sir Thomas More, and, in the second place, that there is no remotely compelling evidence that Sir Thomas More was in fact the author.

I think I can justifiably go further than I did a few paragraphs back, when I described as "very credible" the notion that Cardinal Morton was the real author. I have no direct evidence with which to contradict any of my readers who disagree with me on what I now say, but, in the light of all the circumstantial evidence, I am content to say that I rate it as a practical certainty that Cardinal Morton was the author.

To what extent, therefore, is Shakespeare to blame for his presentation of the vile picture of King Richard III that has so drastically affected the public's opinion of him generation after generation right up to our present day?

As we have now seen, one important fact is that this picture of King Richard III used by Shakespeare is that of a single writer. Another important fact to take into account is that the time when Shakespeare was composing the plays, the early Seventeenth Century, was close enough to the time when King Richard III reigned for him to have easy access to the *very* different reality of that king compared with how he appears in *The History...*

Shakespeare, of course, was far more responsible for creating the picture of King Richard III that is accepted by most people today than were *The History of King Richard III* and *Hollinshed's,* with their, by comparison, tiny readerships; and Shakespeare lived close enough to when King Richard III reigned to make it impossible, in those pre-mass-media days, that the depiction of King Richard in the *History* attributed to Sir Thomas More would be generally accepted then as definitely true or even as reasonably credible.

*   *   *   *   *

So much for our introductory look into the reality of Shakespeare as the historian he holds himself out to be.

Next, it is perhaps worth making the *general* point about his output that, although, at the time that he was writing, he was heir to a Christian tradition that was some sixteen centuries old since its inception, and nine hundred years old in England, and although the plays are written in Christian terminology and often have a Christian background, there is scarcely anywhere in his plays a truly Christian theme to be found. However undisturbing this may be considered to be today, it was revolutionary and subversive of Christian society in his time, and indeed remained unacceptable in principle until a few decades ago.

Let us consider, under this heading, what is the most famous and influential of the plays, and, as we are about to see, has been claimed to be, after the Bible, the most written-about work of Western culture: *Hamlet.*

Chapter 4
The play *Hamlet.*

"*Hamlet*", a Mr. John Carroll informed his readers in an article in the June 1993 issue of an Australian periodical, *Quadrant*, is, apart from the Bible,

> ...the most written-about work of Western culture. It is the most performed play. Indeed in English it has been, from its first appearance, the most regularly performed work in literature. Modern consensus holds that *Hamlet* is the hub of Shakespeare's whole work, the centre from which the other plays reach out as do spokes in a wheel. From 1770 onwards the "Hamlet problem" commenced. For the next century "Hamlet fever" took over Germany. After 1820, throughout Northern Europe, Hamlet scholarship turned into a deluge. As one instance A. A. Raven's bibliography of *Hamlet* literature published between 1877 and 1935 lists over two thousand items.

"My goodness!" – some of my readers are perhaps saying to themselves. The influence of a work as widely performed and read and discussed as that, and of course inevitably featuring prominently in the *curricula* of schools, must be colossal in its degree and extent. We must certainly hope that this influence will be beneficial, in *equal* degree and extent.

Alas!

     *   *   *   *   *

Let us start with a reality that is about as fundamental as any reality about a work of literature could be. In the play *Hamlet*, the beliefs and morals that Christianity taught as certain, and required all Christians to believe, and that almost everyone at that time did believe, simply do not exist. In the philosophy which permeates the play, they are not to be found anywhere.

On the contrary, during the entire course of the play, *everything* is called into doubt except the duty to take revenge, personal revenge, that being of course a "duty" which is the very *antithesis* of Christian belief. In particular, the Christian ethic on murder simply does not feature anywhere in the play. Hamlet's free will consists in his having the choice of whether or not to do the duty to take revenge – a duty which is presented as clear-cut and undoubted.

So that you do not need to rely solely on my judgement on this important subject, let us look at what, in an extremely well-thought-out analysis, the just-quoted Mr. John Carroll has to say on this subject, in the same article.

> Hamlet is, as a hero, the modern individual unconstrained by laws of kin or of state. Everything points in one direction, vengeance.

And that, good reader, is part of what constitutes a *hero*? Let us learn more from Mr. Carroll.

> The conflict is not between two different ethics. There is no suggestion in the text that "Thou shalt not kill" is an overriding ethic. Hamlet is not inhibited by this injunction. He is not in the least concerned about the blood-guilt that might arise from his murdering Claudius. Morality is simply focused on what he sees as his duty: to avenge his father's murder by killing his uncle.

> He is free not to do this duty, however, and it is this freedom that destroys him, and, in the process, all the main characters in the play. The result of Hamlet's dithering is that, in the chaos that ensues, *everyone gets killed*.

> Freedom to choose leaves Hamlet bogged down in his own depression. His thoughts return again and again to suicide, an alternative preferable to having to "grunt and sweat under a weary life". The substance of the play is in fact his own monologue of complaint about life, interrupted here and there by a bit of drama.

What is more, as we learn as we continue with Mr. Carroll:

> After killing Polonius, instead of showing remorse for his unjustifiable murder, Hamlet jokes about mortality. When asked where he has hidden the corpse, he relays that it is at supper, being eaten by maggots.

And in Act V, when he comes upon Ophelia's funeral he jumps into her open grave and asks to be buried with her.

And so on.

And all this is in what Mr. Carroll referred to as "the most written-about work of Western culture, the most-performed play" and all the rest.

Once again: My goodness! *Oh, my goodness*! *What* an influence to subject unsuspecting people to. And let us remind ourselves that impressionable people are, by definition, impressionable, and also that *all* of us are, at least to *some* extent, affected by what we are exposed to.

*   *   *   *   *

Consider now, please, the most famous speech in that play.

"To be or not to be" is simply an eloquently-expressed meditation on suicide.

The traditional Christian position on suicide is that, while those who are tempted to commit suicide may evoke our sympathy and understanding, in no circumstances whatever is committing suicide morally justifiable; also that it is cowardly and despicable. In that speech of Hamlet's there is no indication even of the *existence* of this fundamental Christian position on suicide. Hamlet's sentiment is *solely* on the side of death, "that consummation devoutly to be wished". The *only* argument in opposition to his thoughts of committing suicide is a negative one: fear of the unknown, the "dread of something after death", as Shakespeare puts it in that speech; and even *that* is untraditional and opposed to the Christian position.

There is perhaps just a little more that is worth saying about the few lines comprising this famous minute or two of theatre.

Imagine yourself, please, gracious reader, as a young person born and brought up outside Britain, who is of high intelligence and dedication to scholarship and who from an early age has decided to devote himself or herself to the study of the whole of European literature. Since there is a very large amount of ground to cover, you, this imagined person, decide to be as systematic as possible in how you work at this.

After first tackling the literature of classical Greece and classical Rome, the time in due course comes when you are ready for English literature.

You start with the early Anglo-Saxon authors such as Bede and Chaucer. Soon after that, you are ready to turn your attention, for the first time ever, to the man widely regarded as widely as possibly the greatest of them all: yes, to William Shakespeare. How better to start by going to see the best theatrical production you can find of what you have been told is the most admired of all his plays, indeed possibly the most admired play ever written, *Hamlet, Prince of Denmark*?

If you listen with your wits about you, rather than in a mental daze, it is not long before you start to become puzzled. Far from the play anywhere addressing anything resembling eternal truths, everything – *everything* – is being called into doubt, other than, let us remind ourselves, the need to take revenge. The need to take revenge? And Shakespeare, you have been supposing, was a *Christian* playwright? Patiently you continue to listen, however, in the hope that your impression so far will be put right as things proceed, and then *at last...*

With no idea of what is to come, you are on the edge of your seat with excitement as the lead actor, playing Hamlet and chosen for the role because he is the best actor of your day, opens up the first Scene of Act III with the speech already referred to: probably, as noted earlier, the most famous speech in literature. Its very first line being clearly philosophical in its nature, you can justifiably suppose that the speech will be putting forward for the enlightenment of the audience some important and compelling wisdom, expressed in the most perfect way possible.

The actor advances to the footlights.

"To be or not to be: that is the question," he starts.

Ah, what an excellent opening, you say contentedly to yourself. The greatest of all writers is treating us to a profound ontological dissertation on the subject of Existence, a topic with which the world's greatest philosophers have wrestled since the dawn of recorded history. Wow! This promises to be *really* enlightening.

What is more, you note happily, he is even using the words of Parmenides, who, as you recall, in his analysis of Being and Seeming, said this: "To or not to be: that is the alternative."

This indeed is something to look forward to.

What then follows? You listen in near-disbelief as you gradually become aware that what comes next after those words is nothing more than a trite and thoroughly pernicious meditation, in overblown language, on *suicide*. "To kill myself or not to kill myself: that is the question," is what Hamlet meant by that opening line, as quickly becomes evident. If Hamlet had said exactly that, however, the sentence could hardly have become possibly the most famous in all literature.

Worse is to come. A minute or two later, you learn from what Hamlet says that his *only* reason for deciding *not* to commit suicide, Heaven help us, *is that he is not sure what would come next*, while, at the same time he tells *us* that those of us who would *not* take that step, are *cowards*: "Thus conscience makes cowards of us all."

"Good grief!" I think I hear some of my readers saying to themselves. "The Bard has bothered to bring his hero up to the footlights to waste a couple of minutes of the audience's time with *that*. And can it really be that audiences for hundreds of years have been putting up with it?"

The reality, good readers, is that the most famous speech in the whole of theatrical history is in fact nothing but pretentious and pernicious tripe, which any respected classical dramatist of the distant past would have disgustedly cut his hand off rather than have written, and which would indeed have been booed off the stage by an Athenian audience of classical times. What, from that

opening sentence, we are entitled to assume is going to be a profound philosophical analysis *in fact* amounts to a few trite
thoughts on suicide, and even that is not done in the smallest degree competently – Hamlet's reasoning is intellectually pathetic,
and also thoroughly subversive.

Well, is my jeering justified?

Yes, truly, in the words of the little boy in the classic fairy-tale
by Hans Christian Andersen, the Emperor – representing the auth-
or Shakespeare in this instance – has no clothes. Those who
cannot see this have surely been blinded by of the weight of propaganda.

* * * * *

Is there any room for doubt that Shakespeare is morally subversive? Two facts at least of political history suggest that there
is none. One is that, following the Russian Revolution of 1917,
Hamlet was popular in atheist Russia when the Communist yoke
was at its heaviest and most brutal. The other is that Adolf Hitler
was well known for his enthusiasm for Shakespeare, who was
indeed the only playwright of an enemy country whose works
were not banned by the Nazi regime. To say the least, these are
not good signs. If Shakespeare were an influence for good, the
perverse institutions and philosophies of Communism and Naz-
ism would surely have hated him.

Nor, I suggest, is the philosophy permeating it the only quest-
ionable feature of *Hamlet*. Is it not objectionable that, in addition
to that, it prominently features incest and murder, with the Ghost
in Act 1 describing "the royal bed of Denmark" as "a couch for
damned incest" and Hamlet at the end murdering Claudius with
the words "Here, thou incestuous, murderous, damned Dane"?

* * * * *

So far, so bad. As we are about to see, however, there is, regrettably, even worse to come.

Chapter 5
Two unbelievably horrifying plays.

Titus Andronicus, one of Shakespeare's earlier plays, in fact the fifth one of his output, is surely by any standards a revoltingly degenerate and depraved composition. No *normal* person would be able, even in his wildest imaginings, to come up with a plot such as the one of this play, containing as it does just about every kind of perversion.

It was noted back in chapter 3 that there is not to be found anywhere in Shakespeare's plays a single genuinely Christian theme. For the benefit of those who believe in and care about such things, I consider myself justified in asserting that *this* play, very much to the contrary, is clearly one that could have written by the Devil himself. It must indeed be open to doubt that it is even *possible* that *Titus Andronicus* could have been put together unaided by a purely human mind.

Here is some of what takes place on stage.

   – A young boy is kidnapped and stabbed to death.

   – Another young boy is sacrificed to the gods.

   – Two men tear out a woman's tongue and cut off her two arms so that she cannot divulge, either by speech or writing, what she knows.

   – An old man has his hand cut off, and, together with the heads of his two sons who have just been murdered, this hand is sent to the Emperor.

   – A woman gives birth to a child which, on the grounds that it is black, is evidently proof that it was conceived in adultery.

   – Two brothers are seized and bound with ropes and their throats are cut and their blood streams into a basin.

   – Then their flesh is baked and given to their mother to eat without her realising what she is eating; and after that she is told, and then stabbed to death and thrown among beasts of prey.

There have been scholars who, faced with what this play contains, have refused to believe that it was written by Shakespeare. There is no evidence to support that negative supposition, and I suggest that, even only from what we have seen in these pages so far, it is *in fact* only too credible that he was the author. It is surely arguable, moreover, that the towering genius who wrote the plays of Shakespeare now stands exposed as a thoroughly perverted human being, and that he has, in this play, come out just once, nakedly, in his full true colours.

*   *   *   *   *

Could it, though, be credibly argued that such grossly immoral and perverse content as that of *Titus Andronicus* is so untypical of Shakespeare's plays that we should be entitled to suspect that Shakespeare was not in fact the author of this one?

Would that this were so. Before I start to generalise about Shakespeare's plays, however, there is one more play to look at with some care. To introduce it, I first of all put to my readers this question while the principal features of *Titus Andronicus* are still fresh in our minds. Could anything more horrifying and horrible than this play have ever been written by *anyone*? – other than, possibly, in relatively recent times

I dare say that my readers are supposing that I should not have bothered to ask that question for the purpose of giving a negative answer. And yes, a negative answer is indeed what I cannot give. I really do maintain that, defying belief, or, at the very least, *verging* on defying belief, it can be compellingly argued that the Shakespeare canon *itself* includes a play that offends even more greatly the norms of morality than does *Titus Andronicus*.

*   *   *   *   *

The play that fits this description is *Macb*th* which I have chosen to spell in that strange way, both when using it myself and when quoting others who use it, for a reason that I shall shortly be making clear.

The least objectionable aspect of this play, odious though that aspect would be in any other context, is that it is another of Shakespeare's complete falsifications of history.

Bending over backwards to be completely fair to Shakespeare, which is always my aim, I should make it clear that it is quite likely that he did not know the full extent to which he was falsifying facts when he wrote it. Sources of reliable information about the real Macbeth were not readily available at that time, and the three-volume *Hollinshed's Chronicles* published in 1577, referred to back in chapter 3 in the context of King Richard III, and on which he almost certainly relied to a considerable extent, took an unjustly critical view of Macbeth. *Hollinshed's* went nowhere near as far as Shakespeare in how Macbeth was represented, though, and, as we shall be seeing, cannot be considered to be any sort of reasonable excuse for what the play consists of.

*   *   *   *   *

Very different from the Macb*th depicted by Shakespeare, the *real* Macbeth, whose full name was Macbeth mac Findlaech ("mac" means "son of"), was never other than honourable.

The fact that his mother, Donada, was the daughter of King Malcolm II of Scotland had given him a valid claim to the throne. When King Malcolm II, died in 1034, not Macbeth but another of King Malcolm's grandsons, Duncan I, was elected, and validly so because the High Kings of Scotland, although they needed to be of royal blood in order to be eligible to be monarch, were chosen by election rather than by inheriting as the eldest son.

King Duncan's reign was not a success. During the five years that it lasted, King Duncan fought five wars, and in every one of them suffered defeat. Finally, in 1040, he was killed in battle and Macbeth was elected to the throne in his place.

For seventeen years Macbeth reigned in relative peace and prosperity. A pious man, he undertook during that period a pilgrimage to Rome where, it is recorded, he scattered gifts and money "like seed", an indication of both the security of his position and his prosperity.

Nevertheless, in 1054 the late King Duncan's two sons, Malcolm and Donald Bane, persuaded the English to help them invade Scotland. The English forces were technically the victors, but not decisively enough to result in Duncan's eldest son, Malcolm, replacing Macbeth as king.

Three years later, Macbeth was finally defeated in a battle and killed; and although his place was at first taken by his stepson Lulach, Malcolm succeeded in usurping the throne not long afterwards.

This thoroughly decent man that Macbeth was is represented by Shakespeare as evil beyond the reach of any exaggeration. At the beginning of the play he is at least conscious of his wickedness, but by the end the wickedness has become so extreme and his conscience so dulled that he is completely insensitive to any moral considerations. As he himself, according to Shakespeare, puts it, in Act V, Scene 5, lines 12-14:

I have supp'd full with horrors; direness, familiar to my slaughterous thoughts, cannot once start me.

And, surely not to our surprise, given what we have been learning about Shakespeare as a *consistently* gross falsifier, Malcolm, who in reality was an immoral usurper of the throne, is made into a virtuous hero by the playwright.

Such gross libel of a virtuous man and monarch, and such ennoblement of a man and monarch who was an extreme opposite of virtuous, are of course repulsive to fair-minded people, but they are as nothing by comparison with one *other* notable feature of the play *Macb*th*. This is its intrinsic *malignancy and sinisterness*, which extend far beyond the plot and the people who feature in it.

This particular characteristic of the play is so extraordinary and extreme that I might well be disbelieved by at least some of my readers, if I were to say it only in my own name. I am going to use for the purpose someone who, because he is a professional actor as well as a writer, and his writings would therefore be subject to examination by others in the acting profession, can clearly be trusted in what he says. I have taken the following from chapter 4 of *The Curse of Macbeth and Other Theatrical Superstitions* by Richard Huggett (Picton Publishing, Chippenham, 1981):

Macb*th is the unlucky player of the theatre and has for four hundred years carried in its wake a truly terrifying trail of disaster and bad luck. The play is cursed, and the curse is so strong that it is considered very unlucky to quote from it while inside a theatre. Actors are frightened *even to mention it by name*. If it must be discussed, and this in itself is not encouraged, then it must be done in a roundabout way, and over the years an interesting vocabulary of evasion has gained acceptance. It is talked about as "That Play", or "The Scottish Play" or "The Unmentionable" or "The Caledonian Tragedy" – references that must surely bewilder any backstage visitor.

The bad luck extends to anything that has ever been used for a production of Macb*th, and it is not unknown for an actor to refuse to wear a cloak or helmet if he learns that it was once worn in *That Play*. In the old days of travelling Shakespeare repertory companies, the scenery of the plays would be largely interchangeable, but the costumes, furniture and settings for Macb*th were kept strictly apart. Never, under any circumstances, would a Macb*th throne be used for *King Lear*, *Othello* or *Hamlet*, however hard-pressed the manager was for money, transport or space.

The bad luck also pursues the text if it is quoted in any other play: any playwright who allows his character to say "What bloody man is this?" or "When shall we three meet again?" or "Is this a dagger I see before me?" is asking for trouble and usually gets it.

I happen to have a friend who is a long-standing member of the acting profession, and I checked the above with him. He did not hesitate to agree with it, and volunteered that the play was usually referred to among actors as "the Scottish play". His testimony was perhaps the deciding factor in my resolving that it would be an exercise of due prudence, with nothing to be lost, if I were in most instances to give a non-literal spelling of both the name of the play and the person chiefly featured in it.

To make more vivid and "real" what Huggett has just been saying, it is worth supporting it with one of the many examples that he gives in the book. From the same chapter:

> The Curse is no respecter of amateurs and children. A production at St. John's College in Johannesburg in 1954 ran into an amazing sequence of trouble. A boy called Ivor Sander was selected to play Lady Macbeth but early in the rehearsals he was involved in a car accident and had to withdraw from the play.
>
> His replacement was a sensitive boy called Michael Shuter. Two weeks before the opening he fell from a high window in the middle of the night and broke an arm and a leg; he had apparently been sleepwalking and it was thought that the emotional strain on the part had had an adverse effect on him. Nevertheless, he was able to play it with his leg in plaster and his arm in a sling.
>
> The third climax of trouble concerned the boy, Michael Moreney, who played Macbeth – his mother was killed in a car accident.

Also interesting is an update subsequent to when Huggett wrote that. As was reported in a newspaper very soon after his book was published (reference lost but I have a photocopy of the article), not only does the play consistently bring bad luck, but...

> Huggett first discovered this when he lost all his money and was involved in a car-crash while acting in *Macbeth*. In his words:
>
> > "I have discovered from white witches that Shakespeare's curse in the cauldron scene is a genuine spell, but it can't be taken out because it is pivotal to the play."

While writing the book, all acting offers dried up until the manuscript was completed.

Furthermore, let the reader not suppose, from Huggett's use of the word "superstitions" as part of the title of his book (*...and Other Theatrical Superstitions*), that he does not believe the curse to be a reality and effective. He spends nearly the entirety of his two hundred and fifty-nine-page book showing he very much *does* believe the curse to be a reality, and gives in detail his reasons.

*   *   *   *   *

What possible cause could there be for something so utterly extraordinary and without even the most distant equivalent in any other work of literature of any kind?

It has been firmly believed by many who have done any research on the matter that genuine witchcraft is involved: that somewhere in the play a real curse is hidden in the wording.

This solution will of course be rejected by those whose philosophy rejects completely (a) the supernatural (meaning the intervention of God, as represented by Christian and Judaic religions) and (b) the preternatural (outside the ordinary course of nature and therefore caused by an angelic or a demonic spirit). Such people will, however, find no other solution apart from the supposition that Huggett's summary has nothing to do with reality but is just a baseless superstition.

That supposition – that attempt to escape from the witchcraft-solution – is just flying in the face of facts. I invite you, good readers, to question on this matter the most hard-headed, sober-minded members of the acting profession of your acquaintance. What you will learn is that, *without exception*, no member of their profession refers to "That Play" by its name or quotes from it, and that *all* of them take seriously what Huggett has just summarised, *and* that they do so, they believe, for solidly good reason. And something so universally accepted by everyone of any kind who is knowledgeable on the subject can scarcely be based on nothing.

Furthermore, if such a curse were to feature in any of the plays, *Macb*th* would be much the most likely one for this, because witches actually play a part in it, and even a prominent part, right at the beginning of the very opening scene.

*   *   *   *   *

For those who are interested, I think it worth offering another example of this general phenomenon, this one in a different area of the world of the arts, that of music – in particular, the world of opera and operetta. Although it is a bit of a side-track from our main subject, I think it to be one that our subject's unusual strangeness make it a step worth taking.

The person responsible, what might be called the "Shakespeare", in this instance, is the nineteenth-century German composer Jacques Offenbach, who during his life composed nearly a hundred operettas, many of which have enjoyed great popularity.

The basic facts about Offenbach's operettas are fairly widely known, but, perhaps rather remarkably, I have never seen them better summarised than in the following letter to the *Irish Daily Mail* by one of its readers, E. Felix Schondorfer of Stoke Pages, Bucks, published on 23rd April 2020 and, as will be seen, prominently featuring *The Tales of Hoffmann* in particular. It was submitted in answer to a reader who had put the question: "Are Offenbach's operettas said to be jinxed?"

Jacques Offenbach died before the premiere of *The Tales of Hoffmann*, one of the most significant French operas of the 19th century...

Offenbach was considered to be a *'jettatore'* — someone who has the evil eye. Although partly due to his much caricatured looks – he was skinny with a hooked nose and long blond sideburns – it was also due to the bad luck that surrounded performances of his works.

Ballerina Marie Juliette Estelle Frasey perished in a gas explosion during a dress rehearsal for his ballet *Les Bergères* (*The Shepherds*).

Three years after ballerina Emma Livry premiered the role of Farfalla in his ballet *Le Papillon* (*The Butterfly*), she died after her costume caught fire in a rehearsal.

According to a contemporary report: 'The theatres staging his operas burn down one after the other, the leading ladies feel like they are being strangled and cannot sing anything, the ballerinas twist their arms and legs and lose all their grace."

Support for the belief in Offenbach's fatal influence reached a horrendous peak on 8th December 1881, when at least 386 people awaiting the opening of *The Tales of Hoffmann* at Vienna's Ringtheatre died in a fire caused by a gas leak. One of the victims was teenager Ladislaus Vetsera, brother of Baroness Mary, the mistress of Crown Prince Rudolf of Austria.

Composer Anton Bruckner had planned to attend the performance, but changed his mind at the last minute. He watched the inferno all night from the window of his nearby apartment, an experience which left him deeply traumatised.

The ill-fated work was not staged in the city for the next twenty-five years.

Even after Offenbach's death, superstitious people would not utter his name without raising their index and little fingers, forming a horn to ward off bad spirits.

French literary critic Theophile Gautier was so afraid of Offenbach's malevolent power that if he had to write a review of one of his works, he left a gap for the composer's name, which one of his daughters had to fill in.

As already indicated, I believe that what is related above – extraordinary and of course sinister as it is – gives important credibility to the possibility that the fairly widespread belief that witchcraft is somehow involved in *Macb*th* could be a belief that is based on reality.

At the very least, it seems to me to be sufficiently a possibility to justify the altered spelling that I have made frequent use of in these pages, as seeming to me to be appropriate prudence with nothing to be lost in the exercising of it.

Chapter 6
Noteworthy features of some of the Bard's other writings.

There are two features of Shakespeare's plays that amount almost to a refrain, so frequent is their occurrence.

One is that the plays between them contain no fewer than thirteen suicides and a further *possible* eight suicides. (The actual term "suicide" had in fact not come into existence by the time of Shakespeare, the deed being simply represented by words such "taking one's own life".)

As mentioned in the last chapter, suicide is very much contrary to the traditional Christian position – almost universal in Shakespeare's day – that suicide is a sin, and a very grave sin, and of course one that, unlike any other sin, by its very nature cannot be repented of.

What, furthermore, is considerably worse than suicide merely *taking place*, in play after play in Shakespeare's canon, is that:

on the one hand, it is often – for instance in the suicides of Brutus, Romeo, Ophelia and Cleopatra – depicted as noble and dignified;

while,

on the other hand, it is *nowhere* in the Shakespeare plays represented as other than understandable and forgivable.

It may be granted that in Roman times suicide was widely considered an honourable course to take in certain circumstances. It remains a fact, however:

(a) that in Christian times it could not be acceptable to put such thoughts into the minds of those exposed to his plays without in some way firmly making clear the Christian position;

and

(b) that dwelling on suicide and depicting it as acceptable or better is gravely subversive, which, what is more, is no light matter, because people in a depressed state can easily be pushed into a suicidal direction by thoughts of suicide being put into their minds.

So much for first of the two features referred to above.

The second one, which is bizarre to the extent of even being really weird, in the frequency of its occurrence in Shakespeare's output, is that, in the thirty-seven plays, many of them comedies, no fewer than *seventy-four* smotherings-to-death – *on-stage* smotherings-to-death – take place, starting with Othello's murder of, horrifyingly, his *wife*, Desdemona.

The supposition is verging on inescapable that the author is obsessed with murder, and that he is e*specially* obsessed with murder of a particular kind.

*   *   *   *   *

Still on the subject of violence, there is another feature of the plays that deserves mention, this one scarcely ever, if indeed at all, referred to by commentators on Shakespeare. Although much more subtle, it is arguably even more pernicious than what we have been faced with so far. It is that, in the entire Shakespeare canon, murderers, of which there is a large number, are scarcely ever, if at all, depicted in an any kind of unpleasant light, not even slightly unpleasant. In every single play in which they feature, they are introduced in a simple, matter-of-course way and presented sympathetically. It would not even be an exaggeration to say that they sometimes have some of Shakespeare's best lines.

As an example of such treatment of people guilty of the vilest of crimes, here is *Macb*th*, Act III Scene 1. An attendant brings two murderers to Macb*th, and Macb*th, says to the attendant:

"Now go to the door, and stay there till we call."

A butler enters with a tray of drinks. Macb*th says to him:

"Now go to the pantry and bring more when I ring."

He then turns to the murderers, and says, indicating an easy relationship:

"Was it not yesterday we spent together?"

To that the first murderer responds elegantly:

48

"It was, so please your Highness."

In *Richard III*, Act I Scene 3, the relationship between the King and the murderers is if anything even more relaxed. On their entrance, Richard of Gloucester, as the future King Richard was at that time, treats them as his fellows and equals:

How now, my hardy, stout-resolved mates. Are you going to dispatch this thing?

– "this thing" being the murder of Clarence.

Calling the murderers "mates" is perhaps of special interest here, in that the King Richard that is depicted in the play was ordinarily very much *not* a "matey" person.

More extreme still is what happens in Scene 3 of the same Act. The discussion between the two murderers before they carry out their task could fairly be described as a purely *intellectual* conversation about the morality involved. They look at it from the viewpoints of the kind of murderers who are very much "men in the street" and middle-class businessmen, with the first murderer presenting his thoughts as matters of straightforward logic and the second murderer voicing human feelings of vacillation and, contrary to the norm in Shakespeare, near remorse.

It is worth emphasising that this relaxed approach to professional criminals of the worst kind of all must certainly be relevant when assessing the character of the author. Even if there were only *one* such case in his entire output, Shakespeare's attitude to such criminals could be considered eyebrow-raising. For it to happen repeatedly, with not a single exception anywhere in his plays, is surely sinister, and certainly subversive. I maintain, moreover, that this is not a small matter, and that it is even suggestive that Shakespeare himself may have committed murder and wanted to trample on any beginnings of a guilty conscience.

*   *   *   *   *

Nor is such grossly immoral and perverse content, of which we have just seen some examples, even close to being absent in most of Shakespeare's other plays. Let us look at some other such highlights in the Shakespeare canon. Even his two love-poems, which, for this reason, I have included at the end of this list, are not free from violent deaths.

– As we have seen, *Titus Andronicus*, perhaps most notably of all, has in it instances of rape, murder, incest, vengeance, mutilation, and even of cannibalism.

– *Macb*th*, as we have also seen, is full of murder and vengeance, and of course features witchcraft.

– *King Lear* has murder, vengeance and mutilation.

– *Hamlet* features murder and vengeance, and, at least technically, incest, in the marriage of Hamlet's mother to her brother-in-law.

– *Richard III* of course has multiple killings.

– *Pericles* includes incest as part of the plot.

– People are murdered in each of the three plays *Romeo and Juliet*, *Othello* and *Cymbeline*.

– Perhaps most striking, but seldom noticed: in the much-loved *Romeo and Juliet* every single character without exception behaves with dismaying unpleasantness to other characters in the play.

– Then, too, in Shakespeare's poem *The Rape of Lucrece* vengeance is suggested as a suitable response to the crime of rape referred to in the title, though the poem ends before the vengeance is accomplished.

In what has been listed above, it has emerged that included in the output of the most influential writer of the last four centuries or so are: murder, rape, incest, mutilation, torture, unforgiving vengeance, and witchcraft.

Moreover, just to take one of the categories, there are more than *two hundred and fifty* violent deaths in the Shakespeare canon. That is a figure that ought to make my readers gape. I hope that they are as shocked, even horrified, as they jolly well ought to be.

*   *   *   *   *

So far, I have given what might be called a *representative* list of what I maintain is the unseemly violence that permeates Shakespeare's plays. I shall now expand on the foregoing with a *comprehensive* list of the violent or otherwise unnatural deaths that take place in them. I emphasise (a) that I am doing this simply for the sake of reasonable completeness in my treatment of such an important matter, which indeed is why I include in it plays that have already been looked at, and (b) that I therefore would not consider it objectionable if any readers were to prefer to skip what now immediately follows and move on to the last page of this chapter.

I have arranged what follows in the order that is most widely – though by no means universally – believed to be the chronological order in which the plays were written. Throughout I have used the word "slain" as a convenient technical term for the purpose of indicating death by violence – for instance in battle – that is outside the category of death-by-violence by means of execution, murder or suicide.

– *The First Part of King Henry the Sixth.* The Earl of Salisbury and Sir Thomas Gargrave are both killed by cannonballs. The Earl of Cambridge is executed by being beheaded. The Duke of Bedford and Lord Talbot and his son John are each of them slain. Joan of Arc, who a few centuries later was to become a canonised saint, is burnt at the stake at Rouen at the age of nineteen.

– *The Second Part of King Henry the Sixth.* Roger Bolingbroke is sentenced to death by being hanged, drawn and quartered. That was the form of capital punishment administered for the crime of high treason in England at that time, and this is how it was carried out:

The victim was first dragged, usually by a horse, on a wooden frame to the place where he was to be publicly put to death;

then hanged by the neck until almost dead;

then taken down from the gallows, put on a table, and, while still alive, cut open in the abdomen, after which his intestines and other parts of his body were removed;

and finally, decapitated and the rest of the body "quartered" – that is, hacked into four parts.

In the same play, Lord Say and Sir James Cromer are beheaded, as is the Duke of Suffolk, in his case by pirates. The Rev. John Hume and the clerk of Chatham are hanged. The Rev. John Southwell is sentenced to death but dies before his execution. Margaret Jourdan is burnt at the stake. Duke Humphrey is murdered by either strangling or suffocation. The Earl of Somerset, Lord Clifford, Sir Humphrey Stafford, his brother William Stafford, Thomas Horner, Matthew Goffe and Jack Cade are all slain. An unnamed soldier is killed for no worse crime than calling Jack Cade by the wrong name.

– *The Third Part of King Henry the Sixth.* The pious King Henry VI is stabbed to death in his cell in London – assassinated by Richard, Duke of Gloucester, later King Richard III. Prince Edward and the Earl of Rutland are both stabbed to death. The Duke of Somerset is beheaded. The Marquess of Montague, the Earl of Warwick and Lord Clifford are slain. A father, whom King Henry meets on the battlefield, has been killed by his son, and a different son, whom King Henry also meets, has been killed by his father.

– *The Life and Death of King Richard the Third.* The Duke of Clarence is stabbed and then drowned in a butt of Malmsey, that being a cask of sweet wine that contained also the severed heads of two pigs. The Duke of Buckingham, Lord Hastings, Lord Rivers, Lord Grey and Sir Thomas Vaughan are all beheaded. Lady Anne, after being married to Edward, Prince of Wales, and then to the Duke of Gloucester, who became King Richard III, is poisoned, which, however, does not kill her. King Richard himself, the Duke of Norfolk, Lord Ferris,

Sir Robert Brackenbury and Sir William Brandon were all slain.

– *Titus Andronicus.* No fewer than twenty-one sons of Titus Andronicus are slain. Alarbus is dismembered, after which his entrails are burnt. Mutius, Bassanius, an unnamed nurse, Lavinia, Tamora, Saturninus, and Titus himself are stabbed to death. Martius and Quintus are beheaded. Chicron and Demetrius have their throats cut. The clown is hanged. Aaron is sentenced to death by the new Emperor, Lucius, by being buried up to his chest and then starved to death. Saturninus kills Titus Andronicus after Titus reveals that he has baked Queen Tamora's two sons in the meat pie that Saturninus and Queen Tamora are eating. Queen Tamora is stabbed to death with a butcher's knife by Titus Andronicus, at the gruesome dinner party arranged for Titus.

The violence in the play is actually considerably worse than as represented in that brief summary. For instance, Lavinia, after being raped and mutilated by Tamora's two sons, Chiron and Demetruis, ends up being murdered by her father, Titus of the play's title, to spare her from future shame.

– *The Comedy of Errors.* Aegeon spends the entire play under threat of execution, but in fact no one dies during the course of the play.

– *The Two Gentlemen of Verona.* No one is killed. One outlaw is banished for stabbing a man in the heart.

– *Love's Labour's Lost.* No violent deaths.

– *Romeo and Juliet.* Mercutio, Tybalt and Paris are all slain. Romeo, having heard, wrongly, that Juliet is dead, decides to commit suicide by taking some poison, drinks a fatal potion of the poison, at the same time exclaiming "Thus with a kiss I die" (Act v, Scene 3) and dies next to Juliet, thinking that she is dead, although she is only asleep. Juliet herself, on seeing Romeo dead beside her when she wakes up, picks up Romeo's dagger, kisses him one last time, and then stabs herself to death.

– *A Midsummer Night's Dream.* The mother of a changeling boy, a boy believed to have been deceitfully substituted for another boy, dies while giving birth to that boy. Pyramus and Thisbe (in the play-within-the play) both stab themselves to death.

– *King John.* The Duke of Austria is beheaded. Count Melun is slain, actually dying from his many wounds. Arthur dies from falling from a great height.

– *The Taming of the Shrew.* Luciano is in disguise because he has killed a man. No one dies during the course of the play.

– *King Richard the Second.* The Earl of Salisbury, Thomas Percy, the Earl of Worcester, the Earl of Wiltshire and Sir Bennett Seely are beheaded, as also are Brocas, Bushy and Green (referred to as "creatures to King Richard") and Oxford, Blunt and Kent. The Duke of Gloucester is murdered. Sir Pierce of Exton, mistakenly believing that Henry Bolingbroke, later to be King Henry IV, wishes King Richard dead, goes with two accomplices to King Richard's cell and murders him. The Abbott of Westminster dies of a guilty conscience.

– *The Merchant of Venice.* Antonio is condemned to death by the removal of a pound of flesh, but the sentence is not in fact carried out.

– *The First Part of King Henry the Fourth.* Edmund Mortimer, Earl of March, Shirley, Stafford, Sir Walter Blunt, Henry Percy Hotspur are all slain; Sir Richard Vernon is hanged, drawn and quartered.

– *The Second Part of King Henry the Fourth.* Sir John Colville is sentenced to death.

– *King Henry the Fifth.* With Shakespeare at least having an excuse for *some* of what follows, in that the play was set in wartime:

The Earl of Cambridge, Lord Scroop and Sir Thomas Grey are beheaded.

The Duke of York, the Earl of Suffolk, Sir Richard Ketley, Davy Gam, The Constable of France, Lords Rambures and Grandpré, The Duke of Orléans, the Duke of Bourbon, and several other French noblemen, unnamed, are all slain.

Sir John Falstaff dies of "a burning quotidian tertian" – a fever which comes and goes and which some commentators have supposed to be a well-deserved venereal disease.

Doll dies of "the malady of France", which is *certainly* a venereal disease.

Bardolph and Nym are hanged.

– *Much Ado About Nothing.* No deaths.

– *The Merry Wives of Windsor.* No one is killed. Dr. Caius threatens to cut the throat of Slender but in fact does not do so.

– *The Life and Death of Julius Caesar.* A group of conspirators, led by Julius Caesar's friend, the Roman senator Marcus Brutus, close in on Caesar and stab him to death. Portia, convinced that her husband, Marcus Brutus, will not be able to defeat Anthony and his army, commits suicide in her home in Rome. Marcus Brutus himself commits suicide by falling on his sword, as also do Cassius, Cato and Titinius. Brutus goes so far as to persuade a servant to hold his sword as he throws himself on it.

– *As You like It.* A contestant in a wrestling-match suffers crushed ribs and is expected to die. No one actually does die during the course of the play.

– *Twelfth Night; or, What You Will.* Orsino threatens to kill Cesario and Olivia but does not in fact do so, and no one dies during the course of the play.

– *Hamlet, Prince of Denmark.* Hamlet and Laertes die from being stabbed by poisoned swords. King Claudius, who was Hamlet's uncle, assassinated Hamlet's father by pouring poison, the "juice of cursed hebenon" (1.5.63), into his ear while he was sleeping in his orchard. Polonius, the Lord Chamberlain, acting as a spy for King Claudius, hides behind a curtain in the chamber of Queen Gertrude, Hamlet's mother, in order to listen to her conversation with Hamlet. Hearing a noise, Hamlet stabs through the curtain with a poisoned rapier and then kills him by forcing him to drink from a poisoned goblet. Old Hamlet dies from being poisoned in his ear. Gonzago dies poisoned. Gertrude dies from poison in her drink. Rosencrantz and Guildenstern are put to death. Old Fortinbras is slain. Ophelia, rendered insane by the combination of Hamlet's cruelty to her and the murder of her beloved father, plunges from the branch of a tree into the fast flowing current below. Although the fall was an accident and therefore not a planned suicide, she makes no attempt to save herself, thus turning the accident into a suicide. In the final climatic fencing match, Laertes and Hamlet engage in combat; their rapiers, of which Laertes's is poisoned, are accidentally exchanged; and Hamlet, grasping Laertes's poisoned rapier, wounds Laertes, who dies from the injury.

– *Troilus and Cressida.* Polyxenes, Epistrophus. Cedius, Hector and Patroclus are slain. Pandarus, in the closing words of the play, announces that he will be dying of venereal disease: "Till then I'll sweat and seek about for eases / And at that time bequeath you my diseases."

– *All's Well That Ends Well.* No one dies.

– *Measure for Measure.* Ragozine, weirdly, appears onstage only as a decapitated head. Lucio is hanged, but the play ends before the execution actually takes place. Claudio and Angelo are threatened with execution but end up being pardoned.

– *Othello, the Moor of Venice.* Desdemona is murdered by being smothered by her jealous husband Othello. Emelia is stabbed to death. When Othello learns, after murdering his wife Desdemona, that she had in fact not been guilty of adultery, he commits suicide by stabbing himself to death, and falls down dead beside her. Brabantio dies of grief.

– *Macb*th.* The noble King Duncan of Scotland is stabbed to death by Macb*th. Duncan's two guards are murdered by Macb*th to prevent them from professing that they were not guilty of King Duncan's death. Lady Macbeth, after framing Duncan's servants by placing bloody daggers on them, becomes racked with guilt over the crimes committed by her and her husband, loses her sanity, and eventually commits suicide, as we learn in the closing lines of the play. Banquo is murdered by assassins hired for the purpose by Macb*th. Lady Macduff and her young son are murdered on Macb*th's orders. Macdonald is slain.

– *King Lear.* The Earl of Gloucester dies of a strange mixture – strange indeed to the extent of being possibly unique in literature and with no parallel in history – of shock and joy when his son Edgar reveals to him his true identity as his son. Cordelia is smothered and then hanged. King Lear himself dies of grief. Regan is poisoned to death by her sister, Goneril, after she had set her sights on Edmund, with whom Goneril was having an affair. Goneril stabs herself to death after her depraved plots against her father, King Lear, are exposed. A servant is stabbed to death. The Duke of Cornwall, Edmund and Oswald are slain.

– *Antony and Cleopatra.* Anthony commits suicide by falling on his sword after meeting Cleopatra one last time. Eros also commits suicide by falling on his sword. Cleopatra commits suicide by getting herself bitten by two asps, an asp being one of the many varieties of poisonous snake then and now located in Egypt. Charmian, Cleopatra's lady-in-waiting, commits suicide in the same way. Iras, another of Cleopatra's ladies-in-waiting, falls dead immediately after being kissed goodbye by Cleopatra. Pompey the Great is murdered. Marcus Crassus and Pacorus are slain.

– *The Tragedy of Coriolanus.* In the play's final scene, a group of conspirators, spurred on by Aufidius, the leader of the Volscians, surround Coriolanus and stab him to death.

– *Timon of Athens.* No *definite* violent deaths. Timon, however, after wandering through the wilderness and finding himself unable to live with the general hypocrisy of mankind, is found dead in his cave – at least an *apparent* suicide.

– *Pericles, Prince of Tyr* (supposed by some to have been written jointly with George Wilkins). Antiochus orders the poisoning of Pericles but Pericles escapes. Antiochus and his daughter are both killed by being struck by lightning.

– *Cymbeline.* The Queen, King Cymbeline's wife, wastes away to death in despair over the disappearance of Cloten, her son of an earlier marriage. Cloten is beheaded. Postumus Leonatus dies of grief. The mother of Postumus Leonatus dies during childbirth.

– *The Winter's Tale.* Several characters are threatened with execution, by, respectively: being burnt; being hanged; being flayed alive; and being covered with honey, put on top of a wasps' nest, left there until nearly dead, rescued before actually dying, and then, in Shakespeare's words, "raw as he is, and in the hottest day prognostication proclaims (that can be foreseen), set against a brick-wall, the sun looking with a southward eye upon him, where he is to behold him with flies blown to death." Antigonus is killed by a bear.

– *The Tempest.* No one is killed.

– *King Henry the Eighth, or All Is True.* The Duke of Buckingham is beheaded. Dr. Pace dies of madness.

– *Two Noble Kinsmen* (thought by many to have been written jointly with John Fletcher). Arcite is killed as a result of being thrown from his horse.

– *The Reign of King Edward III*, now generally accepted as part of the Shakespeare canon, although it has been thought by some that, rather, he was a co-author of the play. The King of Bohemia, Prince Edward and Sir Charles of Blois are all slain.

– The poem *Venus and Adonis*. Adonis is killed by being gored by a boar. Furthermore, by the traditionally strict standards of morality of Christianity, the poem can be justly described as unseemly. Commentators have described it as at least verging on pornographic.

– The poem *Lucrece*. After being raped by Tarquin – Lucius Tarqinius, who is a friend of her husband's – the victim, Lucrece, stabs herself to death. Based on early Roman history and originally popularised by the Roman author Ovid, Shakespeare devotes two hundred and sixty-five verses of seven lines each, one thousand eight hundred and fifty-five lines in total, to his much-expanded version. As he tells it, it is an especially revolting story, and it has been classed by some as more than merely *verging* on pornographic.

Other examples of violence in the plays are:

– In *Macb*th*, Macduff and Macb*th fight ferociously in a hand-to-hand combat which ends with Macduff appearing on stage holding Macb*th's head, just severed from his body.

– In *Romeo and Juliet*, when Romeo refuses to fight Tybalt, the cousin of his adored Juliet, Mercutio, enraged that Romeo will not defend his honour, challenges Tybalt to a duel. Romeo attempts to separate the two, but Tybalt fatally wounds Mercutio, who, as he is dying, cries out: "A plague o' both your houses! They have made worms' meat of me." (Act III, Scene 1.)

– Also in *Romeo and Juliet*, after Tybalt kills Romeo's best friend, Mercutio, Romeo challenges Tybalt to a duel, which ends with Romeo leaving Tybalt dead on the ground.

– In *The Life and Death of King Richard the Third*, the Earl of Richmond slays the supposedly villainous King Richard on Bosworth field, in doing so eventually becoming King Henry VII.

– In *The First Part of King Henry the Fourth*, the young Prince Henry and Henry Percy, surnamed and known as Hotspur, engage in a duel on the battle-field and Prince Henry mortally wounds Hotspur, who starts to render one last speech but dies from his wounds without quite completing it.

– In *King Lear*, the malicious Edmund, an illegitimate son of the Duke of Gloucester, and Edgar, a legitimate son of the Duke of Gloucester, engage in a duel in which Edmund is mortally wounded.

– Again expanding on what has already been noted: in *Romeo and Juliet*, Romeo kills Paris, a young nobleman in a duel that takes place next to Juliet's tomb, and, as Paris is dying, promises him that he will lay him beside Juliet.

I submit, in all seriousness, that in its accumulation, and even in some of the individual plays, and indeed even in *some single events* in individual plays, what the catalogue set out above amounts to is, clearly, the product of someone who is gravely perverted in character, even sinisterly so.

*   *   *   *   *

Thus Shakespeare as he really is, and I hope with the result of at least some of my readers grinding their teeth in disgust.

In more detail: grinding their teeth at the reality that it is *a plain fact* that there is not *a single truly wholesome play or other piece of literature* to be found *anywhere* in his works, whether in the plays or the various pieces of verse; *and* at the reality that there is a very great deal in them that is grossly unwholesome.

Can that be excused on such grounds as that the works of Shakespeare are "great literature"? Given the powerful effect of compelling literature of any kind on those who are exposed to it, I emphatically deny that it can.

Moreover, all the more firmly would I deny any claim, if made, that such an approach to the writing of plays is intrinsic to success in the profession of playwright, and that those whose works do not offend against morality and seemliness cannot expect to be successful. Even in our own era alone, beginning at the end of the 19th century, playwrights have enjoyed all the success that they could wish for without, at least for the most part, having offended against good taste, obvious examples being Gilbert of the Gilbert and Sullivan partnership, Bernard Shaw, Terence Rattigan and Noel Coward.

In the words, once again, of Congressman John Randolph of Roanoke:

Like rotten mackerel by moonlight, he shines and he stinks.

Given that, as already noted, what we read in books and what we watch in the theatre can be expected to have at least *some* effect on us, and given that the more powerfully it is written and presented, the greater the effect will be, can it be seriously argued that what I have been outlining in the last few paragraphs is suitable material to expose even adults to – let alone to put in front of children, for whom in our present day Shakespeare is routinely part of education?

Chapter 7
Shakespeare's Sonnets.

A sonnet is a piece of verse – most often a love-poem – consisting typically of fourteen lines of which the first twelve lines rhyme alternately (the first line with the third line, the second line with the fourth line, and so on) and the last two rhyme with each other. William Shakespeare wrote one hundred and fifty-four sonnets in accordance with this system; and, as one would expect of him, they are faultlessly composed and beautifully worded.

In our present era it is probable that most readers will not be shocked by what I am now going to point out. From the time that Shakespeare was writing until well into the twentieth century, however, very many who looked at those pieces of verse with reasonable care certainly would have been.

If you look at the sonnets one by one, you will find that, as is widely agreed by commentators on Shakespeare, every single one of the first one hundred and twenty-six of them is addressed to a young member of the male sex, who is referred to in such terms as "Fair Youth". In the past this was considered unseemly, to say the least, and from time to time some of the sonnets were actually censored out of publications of his works.

Rather than speak in my own name – which, as already mentioned, I like to avoid doing when I reasonably can when dealing with controversial matters, preferring to quote someone else whom I am happy to endorse – I shall now reproduce part of an article by a columnist, Katherine Craik, that appeared in the *Times Literary Supplement* in its issue of 17th April 2020:

> The sonnets which now score most highly in terms of lovability, such as "Shall I compare thee to a summer's day", were excluded from early collections and are nowhere to be found in the *First Folio* of 1623. While the plays flourished in multiple 17th-century editions, the sonnets faded into obscurity.

As Shakespeare's canonisation continued into the 18th century, the sonnets began to fare better. Nevertheless, the fundamental problem remained that Shakespeare was addressing a man, and dealing frankly with same-sex desire. Early editors had to perform increasingly elaborate contortions to get around this uncomfortable truth.... Victorian bardolators were equally vexed by the sonnets' "queerness", but worked more determinedly to domesticate it.

I now quote from the Introduction of an edition of *Shakespeare's Sonnet's*, edited by W.J. Rolfe, A.M. (1905, American Book Company). From page 22:

After arranging the first 126, or all that he regarded as addressed to "Mr. W. H." or the poet's male friend, he appended those written to the "dark lady"...

It is very doubtful whether certain sonnets in the first group (1-126) properly belong there. Some of them appear to have been addressed to a woman rather than a man — for instance, 97, 98, 99, etc. Of course everybody familiar with the literature of that time knows, as Dyce remarks, that "it was then not uncommon for one man to write verses to another in a strain of such tender affection as fully warrants us in terming them amatory." Many of Shakespeare's sonnets which he addressed to his young friend are of this character, and were it not for internal evidence to the contrary might be supposed to be addressed to a woman. But Sonnets 97, 98, and 99 could hardly have been written to a male friend even in that day. Look at 99, for example:—

The forward violet thus did I chide:
Sweet thief, whence didst thou steal thy sweet that smells,
If not from my love's breath? The purple pride
Which on thy soft cheek for complexion dwells
In my love's veins thou hast too grossly dyed.
The lily I condemned for thy hand,
And buds of marjoram had stol'n thy hair;
The roses fearfully on thorns did stand,
One blushing shame, another white despair;
A third, nor red nor white, had stol'n of both,

And to his robbery had annex'd thy breath;
But, for his theft, in pride of all his growth
A vengeful canker eat him up to death.
More flowers I noted, yet I none could see
But sweet or colour it had stol'n from thee.

Rolfe's Introduction then continues:

If this sonnet were met with where we had no external evidence that it was addressed to a man, could we have a moment's hesitation in deciding that it must be addressed to a woman? Even in Elizabethan times, when extravagant eulogies of manly beauty were so common, do we find the poet dwelling upon his "love's breath" or the "lily" whiteness of his hand? From first to last, the sweetness and loveliness described in the verses are unmistakably feminine.

Indeed a magazine article by a columnist Charlotte Chauvette, is actually titled "Defining Early Modern Pornography: The Case of Venus and Adonis" (as readers may recall, *Venus and Adonis* was a narrative poem by Shakespeare), featured in the Winter 2012 edition of *The Journal for Early Modern Cultural Studies* (volume 12, number 1, University of Pennsylvania Press). Starting on page 29:

The poem was incredibly popular in its day, going through six editions before 1599, and inspired numerous imitations on its erotic theme. Venus and Adonis's notoriety eventually earned the poem a place on the library shelf of "Love's Academy", a repository of arousing books imagined by the author of the pseudonymous pseudo-sexual advice-pamphlet, *The Practical Part of Love* (1660). The poem's popularity among "amorous young students and courtiers," Katherine Duncan-Jones notes, was so well established even by 1600 that references to the poem as a young man's "sex manual", or as a "handbook for wooers", became a running joke in the Jacobean theater (496–97)... Concerns about the poem's popular audience become palpable in the early 19th-century writing of Y.J., who encourages readers to revisit the poem and celebrates Shakespeare's aesthetic achievements, but warns that the poem "is not a proper book to be in all hands"...

Four lines of the poem (lines 231-234) are so shocking by traditional Christian standards that I am not going to reproduce them here.

Chapter 8

A glance at a few of Shakespeare's more famous sayings.

Before we leave the written works of Shakespeare's, one last feature of them that is well worth looking at with some care is the wise sayings with which, according to the claims of his proponents, his output is so lavishly filled.

I should not dream of disputing that his sayings include a fair number that *are* very wise, and well expressed too. I am delighted to be able to say that, if only to show that I am not dictated to by prejudice.

Take, for instance:

> Who steals my purse steals trash; 'tis something, nothing; 'twas mine, 'tis his, and has been slave to thousands; but he that filches from me my good name robs me of that which not enriches him and makes me poor indeed.

That is the natural law memorably expounded. The same can be said of:

> Sweet are the uses of adversity, which like the toad, ugly and venomous, wears yet a precious jewel in his head.

The same, too, can be said of countless others of Shakespeare's sayings.

Not that it matters, but because it does not seem to be widely recognised, it is perhaps worth mentioning that by no means all of them are original and that many of his most famous "quotables" are borrowings, often in slightly different wording, from the classics.

We have already seen one example of this: the famous "To be or not to be…" that is a straightforward pilfering – transposed into a subversive context and trivialised – of the classical Greek philosopher Parmenides's "To be or not to be, that is the alternative". Here, out of very many that could be given, are two more examples:

– Falstaff's "the better part of valour is discretion" in *Henry IV Part I* comes from Euripides' "To my mind discretion is valour" in his *The Suppliants* (510).

– "Though this be madness there is method in it" (*Hamlet* II:2) reflects exactly Horace's "He seems to be insane with some deliberation".

As I have just indicated, I have no objection to Shakespeare's reliance on the classics for a large proportion of his gems of wisdom, On the contrary, as I think I have made clear, I wish Shakespeare really *had* been a traditionalist, rather than a whole-hearted subversive who dressed up his pernicious messages in the sheep's clothing of a certain amount of timeless sagacity.

That said, however, it is surely worth mentioning that I think that many of his most fervent admirers are not aware of the extent of his borrowings and therefore rate him as a more important philosopher than merely someone who was, to a considerable extent, a copier of other people's brilliant shafts of wisdom. It is difficult to feel quite the same about one of his memorable quotations if one is told: "Yes, and as with many of his other nuggets, exactly the same thing was said just as well by such-and-such a classical author about two thousand years ago, and when *he* said it, it was probably original."

*   *   *   *   *

In what I have said so far in this chapter, I have *not* intended to give any sort of indication that I consider *all* of William Shakespeare's famous sayings to be pearls of wisdom, or even remotely acceptable, let alone of any value.

Consider, for instance, this, said by Polonius in *Hamlet*'s Act I, Scene 3:

To thine own self be true.

Undoubtedly those words *sound* good. Even to hear them or to read them can prompt the heart to beat more courageously.

But in what direction? Did Christ teach that or anything like it? He did not. On the contrary, He taught, and Christianity has consistently taught:

    – that the key to holiness and happiness lies in generous *self-renunciation*;

    – and that, for everyone, the essential personal battle consists, *not* of being *true to self*, which regrettably is all too easy,

    – *but*, rather, of the *conquest and control* of self, of the elimination of selfishness, and of the struggle to suppress our innate tendency *to indulge and assert* self.

Is not something like "To thy duty be true, no matter what the cost to self" a concept that is potentially much more fruitful in its influence?

It would not, I think, be far-fetched to think that that *single* remark of Shakespeare's, world famous as it has been for so long, must have done incalculable damage during the course of history. I myself have heard it expressly used as an argument to justify taking the wrong decision, the decision to allow *feelings* to dictate an attractive-appearing though patently unwise course of action, rather than make the sacrifice of allowing *reason and duty* to decide.

Certainly the sentiments contained in it rule triumphantly today. We live in an era characterised by self-indulgence, self-expression, self-made ethics, and so on. And I submit that, even if that were the *only* subversive saying of Shakespeare, which, as we are about to see, certainly is not, it would be enough to make it only too possible that his influence was disastrous; for it is a truism that a spoonful of deadly poison is more dangerous when concealed in a large glass of refreshing water than when it is offered neat.

Here are a few more examples:

    – *Hamlet* again, in Act III, Scene 1: "Conscience does make cowards of us all," clearly implying that there are occasions where one cannot be expected to follow one's conscience.

– *Hamlet* yet again, in Act I, Scene 4: "It is a custom more honour'd in the breach than the observance." Can it really be that those of us who read and/or attend the Shakespeare plays are expected to agree that we *honour* a good and respected custom if we act in a way that is in contradiction to it?

– *Henry IV Part I* Act I, Scene 2:

Poins: "How agrees the devil and thee about thy soul, that thou soldest him on Good-Friday last for a cup of Madeira and a cold capon's leg?"

Prince Henry "Sir John [Sack] stands to his word. The devil shall have his bargain, for he was never yet a breaker of proverbs: he [Sir John] will give the devil his due."

Yes, we are being invited to suppose that, if someone makes a pact with the devil, he is morally obliged to act in accordance with that pact, rather than, wholeheartedly and with determination, to *renounce* it.

– *Henry IV, Part II*, Act IV, Scene 5: "The wish is father to the thought."

In full:

Henry V: "I never thought to hear you speak again."

Henry IV: "Thy wish was father, Harry, to that thought. I stay too long by thee, I weary thee."

There we are, disastrously, led to believe that it is acceptable to be guided in our thoughts and our duties and our actions, *not* by what we *ought* to do, but by what we *want* to do?

I hope that I have given enough evidence to make my point. Please be assured that there is more that I could offer. Anyway, because of the enormous influence wielded by Shakespeare on countless people, even just one all by itself would have been enough for what I have been trying to show.

Tragically, Shakespeare was as unsound – to put it delicately – on matters of morals as he was on the many other aspects of him that we have been looking at in these pages.

*   *   *   *   *

69

To repeat *yet again* what John Randolph said of a fellow member of the U.S. House of Representatives in the eighteenth century:

Like rotten mackerel by moonlight, he shines and he stinks.

Taking all that I have said about Shakespeare so far, which, as I have said, I give my assurance is only scratching the surface, are my readers now happy for me to apply those words of Randolph's to Shakespeare?

*   *   *   *   *

All in all, that brings to an end what I consider to be my mission to enlighten open-minded readers as to the *reality* of what William Shakespeare gave to the world almost exactly four centuries ago.

PART II

The authorship of the works of William Shakespeare: no less controversial a topic.

Chapter 1

The overall problem of Shakespeare's real identity.

Sweet Swan of Avon! What a sight it were
To see thee in our waters yet appear...

Thus wrote Ben Jonson, a popular playwright of the same era, in his Preface to the edition of the works of William Shakespeare that was published in 1623 and is known as the First Folio. Derived from those words of Jonson's is the title "the Bard of Avon" by which the person responsible for those works is popularly known. And my goodness! No one was better placed to know who the author of Shakespeare's works was than Ben Jonson, as will become evident as we continue, occasionally quoting him further.

*   *   *   *   *

I have refrained thus far from attributing the authorship of the so-called works of Shakespeare *expressly* to the man commonly referred to as William Shakespeare. As I made clear that I should be doing when I was starting chapter 1 of PART I, I have been using the name William Shakespeare purely for practical convenience, rather than as any sort of indication that I suppose a person with the name William Shakespeare was the real author. The time has now come to address this topic directly.

I shall say at the outset that I shall be continuing this "refraining", and also that I shall end up giving an answer to the question of who the real author was that is,

not merely *possible*,

or even *highly probable*,

but *definitely* and *undoubtedly* correct

– *demonstrably* so.

*   *   *   *   *

There are those who maintain that it is of no real importance who the author of the works attributed to William Shakespeare was, and that, rather, what matters, and *all* that matters, is that we have his plays, his sonnets and his other poems.

Surely this is less than completely rational, though. If the world has been deceived as to who the author was, two things of which we can be certain are:

- in the first place, that there was a *reason* for the deception;
- and in the second place, that we cannot judge the importance or otherwise of the reason until we know what this reason is.

I invite my readers, therefore, to examine the matter with me with due attentiveness. I think I can justifiably assure them that, if they do, the result will be enthusiasm for those who are open-minded and revulsion for those who are closed-minded!

I start with some pertinent information together with some pertinent questions, numbered for convenience.

1. According to the author Sir E. Maunde Thompson, G.C.B., in Chapter III page 58 of the book *Shakespeare's Hand in the Play of Sir Thomas More* (Cambridge University Press, 1923), there are only six surviving authentic signatures of "Shakespeare", all of which were used in the signing of legal documents or depositions: Willm Shakp, William Shakspēr, Wm Shakspē, William Shakspere, Willm Shaksper. *Not once* did he use the spelling "William Shakespeare".

Furthermore, I have the backing of an extremely learned Shakespeare scholar, Professor A. J. Pointon, former Director of Research at Portsmouth University, when I say firmly that all of those spellings were pronounced differently from how "*Shake*speare" would be pronounced, since in every case the first part of the name would be pronounced "shack", rather than "shake". (*The Man Who Was Never Shakespeare* by A. J. Pointon, Parapress, Tunbridge Wells, 2011: page 22.)

Just in case anyone should want additional confirmation of this important point, Here, on the same subject is Mr. William Edwards in his *Shaksper Not Shakespeare* published in 1900:

"The name Shakespeare is quite different etymologically (in word-derivation) and orthographically from Shagsper or

Shakspere or Shaxpeyr of Shaksper. It is not in evidence that any author lived in the age of Queen Elizabeth whose family and baptismal name was William Shakespeare or Shake-speare. There is no such historical man – no known individual who bore that name."

Why, then, has the author from the very beginning been called variously "Shakespeare" and "Shake-speare", the name on the published folios, when the family of Will Shaksper of Stratford, although its members, at various times, spelt that name in about sixty different ways, and *never once* spelt it in that way?

2. How can it be that Will Shaksper of Stratford *never once* spelt his name as Shakespeare or Shake-speare; not even after the works bearing that name had been published and others were using that spelling when writing about him? For that matter, why did he hyphenate his name when attaching it either to the Sonnets or to the many Quartos in which some of the plays appeared before the publication of the all-containing First Folio in 1623?

3. How is it possible that not a single item of correspondence of any kind from, or relating to, such a prominent and notable person as the author of the Shakespeare plays, popular as they were, survives?

4. How is it that Ben Jonson, who, as we have just seen, wrote admiringly of him in his Preface to the works published in 1623, and, as will become evident, must have known him personally, never made any reference to his death?

5. What can be the explanation of the extraordinary fact that neither the father nor the daughters of one of the greatest literary figures in history could either read or write? (Occasionally each of them needed to put a signature to an attesting-document, and, in every case without exception, no actual *signature* was put, but only a mark.)

This fact about the daughters in particular, incidentally, is sufficient, *even by itself*, to rule out even the slenderest possibility that the Stratford-born Will Shaksper could be the author of Shakespeare's works. The notion that a highly intelligent and well-educated man would bring up his children completely unable to read or write is simply absurd.

6. How is it that, as all Shaksper's biographers who address the point accept, no surviving specimen of his handwriting is to be found in any of the Shakespeare archives?

7. How is that neither in his lifetime nor in his last will-and-testament did Will Shaksper make any reference to any ownership of or connection with his plays and sonnets? Is there any precedent in the history of literature for that?

8. How is it that the will-and-testament of the man whose very life must have been made up of books – not only books written in English, but also books written in, for instance, Greek, Latin, French, Italian – makes no reference to a collection of books in his ownership, and indeed no reference even to a single book of any kind? That would not necessarily be of any significance today, when books are available cheaply and in profusion; but in his day, and for some considerable time afterwards, it must be doubtful if there is any precedent for *that* in a major literary figure.

9. Whatever allowance we might make for the fact that he was a genius to transcend all geniuses, how, even so, was someone with his social, educational and financial background able to acquire all the knowledge of various kinds that he displayed in his writings?

It is worth pausing briefly in this list of questions in order to elaborate a little on that last question. The fact is that *intrinsic* genius, however great, will only take those who possess it so far. It gives a person the power to *acquire* knowledge, *but genius is not knowledge itself*, and is not, *by itself*, sufficient to p*rovide* knowledge. Genius has never taught a person to conjugate a

Greek verb or even to recite a multiplication table. Textbooks such as books of grammar, classroom-lessons or private lessons and so on are needed as well. As one admirer of Shakespeare, as I shall now return to calling our author, aptly summarised this particular problem:

> It would require not genius but Divine inspiration to enable a young provincial apprentice, who had passed through call-boy to play-actor and who had picked up a few crumbs of education at the Stratford Free School (where, by the way, he had, it would seem, given no indications of genius what-ever)... to write of all things under Heaven as never man wrote before or since. (*Avalanche of Falsity* by Paul Hemenway Altrocchi, M.D. (Universe, Indiana, 2014).)

Moreover, scholarly books dealing with Shakespeare's works have been written that, as the authors of some of those books have justifiably maintained, make it clear that he might well have actually *been* a soldier, a sailor, a lawyer, an astronomer, a doctor, a printer, and, perhaps most obviously, a courtier, so extensive and deep was his knowledge in those fields.

I return to the numbered questions, with three more to offer.

10. How did this author acquire an intimate knowledge of places that someone living the sort of life that he did could never have visited? Books have been written to demonstrate that he must have personally *visited* Scotland, highly improbable in the light of what is known of Shaksper's life, *and* – unlikely for someone of his background to the extent of being arguably *impossible* if it were not actually the case – Germany and Italy too.

Specifically, how is it that he was able to display an *accurate* knowledge of several towns in northern Italy – Padua, Verona, Milan, Mantua, and especially, of course, Venice, which, as people who know Venice have pointed out, he writes of as only someone closely acquainted with that city could have written? There were no guide-books in those days, of course, and, even if there had been, knowledge passed on by any such means does not enable one to write about it as though one has actually *been* there.

11. How did his extraordinary *learnedness* that is such a prominent feature of all his works come about?

Let us start with the Latin and Greek element of that learnedness.

Considerable competence in both those languages he certainly had. Yes, as is well known, Ben Jonson did take it upon himself to say of him "Thou hadst small Latin and less Greek", but that must have been with tongue in cheek, since there is not the slightest doubt that our author knew Latin very well indeed.

I do not expect you to take my word for this. I call to witness Professor Churton Collins, a professor of English who was a nineteenth-century scholar and literary critic of sufficiently exceptional distinction to have merited entries devoted to him in *Encyclopaedia Britannica*, *Chambers Biographical Dictionary* and other such reference books, and who, interestingly in the present context, always fully accepted that the author of the works of Shakespeare was indeed the man born in Stratford. In his book *Studies in Shakespeare* (Archibald Constable & Co, London, 1904), Professor Collins says on page 16:

> His familiarity with the Latin language is evident:
>
> first, from the fact that he has, with a minute particularity of detail, based a play on a poem of Ovid and on a comedy of Plautus, both of which he must have read in the original as no English translations, so far as we know, existed at the time;
>
> secondly, from the fact that he has adapted and borrowed many passages from the classics, which were almost certainly only accessible to him in the Latin language.

To that I can add, as a once-reasonably-competent Latinist myself, that to be able to read the classical Latin authors without having to struggle constantly to understand the text needs a fairly exceptional degree of scholarship.

For further information on this aspect of Shakespeare, hold your breath as I pass on the following information given by the learned Lord Sydenham of Combe and Mr. H. C. Crouch Batchelor in their jointly-written booklet *The "Shakespeare" Myth – a Challenge* published in 1924.

According to them, the plays show beyond doubt that our author was very familiar with the works of: Aristotle, Plato, Euripides, Sophocles, Pliny, Lucretius, Tibellus, Statius, Plutarch, Seneca, Tacitus, Ovid, Virgil and Cicero; and this, they inform their readers, was despite many of those classics not yet having been translated in Shakespeare's day.

Already that list is sufficient evidence that the author's familiarity with both classical Latin and classical Greek could not be even a remote possibility for someone with the limited education that was the most that a Stratford schoolboy could have had access to. The position, furthermore, can be made even worse for the "Stratfordians". Here is Professor Churton Collins again in the same essay; and it is worth stressing that he is all the more powerful a witness for our purpose in that he indicates consistent dislike of what he finds himself compelled to say, because, remaining – as he somehow manages to persuade himself to do – a Stratford-Shakespearean, he is confronted with what is, on the face of it, an absurdity: the notion that someone of Shakespeare's background – which meant leading the only life that someone of that background could have led – *could* have this competence.

> Nor must we forget the many curious parallels between his [Shakespeare's] play on words, his studied use of paronomasia, of asyndeton, of onomatopoeia, of elaborate antithesis, of compound epithets, of subtle periphrasis, and above all his metaphors – with those so peculiarly characteristic of the Attic dramas.
>
> I have not space to illustrate, but it is the extraordinary analogies – analogies in sources, in particularly of detail and point, and in relative frequency of employment, presented by his metaphors to the metaphors of the Attic tragedians –

that I find the most convincing testimony of his familiarity with their writings.

Well, ladies and gentlemen, my good readers, how *did* Shakespeare achieve a level of scholarship that was exceptional to such a degree as that, and indeed would be notable even in people renowned for their learning and educational qualifications? How *did* he achieve this in his relatively brief spell at Stratford Free School, where no evidence of any particular intelligence on his part is recorded, and indeed where his record, if he was there at all, is so unremarkable that there is no *extrinsic* evidence that he was actually educated there? How *did* someone with the range of knowledge that a Stratford schoolboy could acquire in a few short years, manage to put together a literary output that would be beyond the reach of many, indeed most, professors at the Oxford and Cambridge universities.

Are any of my readers still resistant to what I maintain is clear and inescapable reality? I add to their problem with another of the numbered questions.

12. How did he acquire the astonishing amount of technical *legal* knowledge that is everywhere evident in his works?

It is worth elaborating on this.

Those of us who are not lawyers can have no conception of how impossible it is for a layman – someone without specialist legal training – to handle legal jargon as Shakespeare did. We can, however, perhaps get *some* idea by considering an analogy.

Imagine someone writing a novel based on life at a school where we ourselves had been but who himself or herself had not been at school there. It might be possible for such an author not to make any definite mistakes in depicting life at that school, because the author could show what had been written to someone who had had been there and ask for it to be checked and for any errors to be corrected. We can, nevertheless, safely guarantee that we should know if the book had been written by someone who *had* been there. There would be endless tiny details – such as the school song, the school's geography, the slang language peculiar to it, and so on – which such a person would include and which could never occur to someone who was basing the novel purely on research.

Similarly, people not educated and trained in the law can have not even a remote conception of the extent to which Shakespeare's works are punctuated with the "lawyer-speak", because non-lawyers very often would not recognise a particular wording as legal language.

Yet the fact that the works of Shakespeare *are* permeated by legal allusions and terminology that are inevitably foreign to the layman, and yet are used with unerring accuracy, has been confirmed by representatives of the highest eminence in the legal profession, and not just by one such person but by many.

For as authoritative a witness as anyone could reasonably want, here is Lord (John) Campbell, one of the most distinguished lawyers of the nineteenth century, and successively Lord Chief Justice and Lord Chancellor, and all the more interesting for our purpose in that, as in the case of the book by Professor Churton Collins of which I made use earlier in this chapter, his book on the subject is a wholehearted defence of the authorship of Stratford's Shaksper (referred to by him throughout as Shakespeare).

Dealing first with whether a layman can converse credibly in legal terminology, he says on page 109 of his *Shakespeare's Legal Acquirements Considered* (D. Appleton and Co.,1859) – the emphasis added is mine:

> Let a non-professional man, however acute, presume to talk law, or to draw illustrations from legal science in discussing other subjects, *and he will speedily fall into laughable absurdity.*

Lord Campbell supported that with examples taken from twenty-six of the plays and several of the sonnets.

And this is how, on the previous page of the same book, he spells out what he sees as the reality:

While novelists and dramatists are constantly making mistakes as to the laws of marriage, of Wills and inheritance, to Shakespeare's law, lavishly as he expounds it, there can be neither demurrer [legal objection], nor bill of exceptions, nor writ of error.

That is to say: only a trained lawyer with plenty of *practical* experience in the legal profession could have written as Shakespeare did in his plays.

Do any readers harbour even the slightest doubt that what Lord Chief Justice and Lord Chancellor Lord Campbell says so emphatically above is an inescapable and unquestionable reality? In my view without necessity, but just in case it could make a difference, I call upon, for additional authority, a further two learned experts, Professor B. J. Sokol and his wife Dr. Mary Sokol, both of them teachers at London University.

In their Introduction at the beginning of their jointly-authored 500-page book *Shakespeare's Legal Language – A Dictionary* (Athlone Press, London and New York, 2000 and 2004) what they say includes this:

Of the thirty-seven Shakespeare plays considered in this Dictionary, thirty-five contain the word "judge" and thirty-five the word "justice"... Reference to a trial appears one or more times in twenty-five of Shakespeare's plays, and many contain or describe trial scenes.

The *sole* Shakespeare play text that contains neither the words "judge" nor "trial" is *The Taming of the Shrew,*... but *The Taming of the Shrew* contains marriage and marriage settlements at its core. In fact the terms related to the legalities of marriage constitute the largest thematic cluster in this Dictionary. It is indeed possible to argue that Shakespeare was law-obsessed...

The overall impression given by this Dictionary may well contradict frequently-reiterated claims that Shakespeare's interest in law was at best superficial, and that Shakespeare exploited legal ideas, circumstances and language with no regard for any factor aside from "poetic" effect. It is our view, derived from cumulative evidence, that, on the contrary, Shakespeare shows a quite precise interest in the capacity of legal language to convey matters of social, moral and intellectual substance.

Furthermore, what Lord Campbell, Professor Sokol and Dr. Sokol say is confirmed by a string of lawyers who thought the matter remarkable enough to be worth going into print about, both in books and in a long-running periodical called *Baconiana* that was published regularly from 1886 to 1999 by an organisation called the Francis Bacon Society.

And now, to the last of the thirteen questions that I referred to as my "pertinent questions":

13. How could it have come about that, ten years after the death of William Shakespeare, the renowned Ben Jonson, another of the leading playwrights and poets of the time, made a list of the great men of his acquaintance that included *no mention* of Shakespeare even though his involvement with him was so close that, as we shall be seeing in chapter 10, he wrote an introductory poem that featured prominently.

*   *   *   *   *

Sceptical writers have suggested that Shakespeare might have been a clerk in a lawyer's office – possibly in Stratford before he came to London, possibly after arriving in London. However plausible that might seem to a layman, legal experts, with only one exception that I have come across in my researches, have found the notion absurd.

In the first place, they say,

(a) no young man could possibly have worked in a lawyer's office without being called upon *continually* to act as a witness, and therefore leaving traces of his name in many places for researchers to uncover without difficulty; and

(b) the names of witnesses and persons otherwise involved in legal proceedings in past centuries are peculiarly immune to historical loss, owing to the great care with which legal papers need to be, and are, preserved over long periods of time.

In the second place, they continue, there is not, in all that is known about Shakespeare, a single fact or incident, or even rumour or tradition, however faint, which supports the notion of a clerkship in a lawyer's office.

In the third place, for what is the most obvious objection of all, I quote a fervent admirer of Shakespeare's, Gerald Massey:

> The worst of it is for the theory of his having been an attorney's clerk, that it will not account for his insight into law; his knowledge is not office sweepings, but ripe fruits, mature, as though he has spent his life in their growth. (Quoted on page 377 of *The Shakespeare Problem Restated* by G. G. Greenwood (John Lane and Bodley Head, London, 1907).)

*   *   *   *   *

I could in fact ask other "impossible-to-answer" questions too; but I think that it is now time to conclude with a comprehensive summary of the apparent Shakespeare "impossibles" that is given in a comprehensive two-volume book, *The Authorship of Shakespeare*, by Nathaniel Holmes, an impressive man of letters of his time, which was the late-nineteenth century. What he says is important for our purposes because his range of scholarship far exceeds mine and he is able to offer much more information than I should have been able to without his help.

What now follows comes from near the beginning of the first volume, a section of the opening chapter that is sub-headed "His learning". Some of it, as of course is to be expected, amounts to repetition of some of what I have just been saying, but, because of the great importance of this aspect of the authorship of the works of William Shakespeare and the extent and depth of Holmes's knowledge relating to the subject, I think it best to give Holmes a reasonably complete "say".

From, therefore, chapter one of volume I of *The Authorship of Shakespeare* by Nathaniel Holmes (Houghton, Miffles and Company, Boston and New York, 1887).

For the learning of Shakespeare, his knowledge of history and of the manners, customs, and literature of the ancients, his acquaintance with foreign languages, his natural science and metaphysical philosophy, his skill in both the medical lore of his time and the laws of England, his familiarity with the manners of the Court and high society, the vast range of his observation in all the realms of nature and art, as well as in all that pertains to the civil state, or to the affairs of private life, or to the characters, passions, and affections of men and women, or to human life and destiny, the subtle profundity of his intellect, and his extraordinary insight into all the relations of things, – all this and much more must wholly depend upon the argument to be drawn *from the internal evidence contained in the writings themselves*, even though this not only is not supported in any other way, but, rather, is for the most part *absolutely contradicted* by the known facts of his personal history.

It is apparent that this argument can have no weight whatever in favour of the William Shakespeare [sic – there was of course no person of that name. – N.M.G.] of Stratford.

The learning and philosophy of these plays attributed to Shakespeare have been a matter of wonder to editorial critics and a stumbling-block to all great writers who have treated of the subject. Even Dr. Samuel Johnson, in his *Preface to the Plays of William Shakespeare,* was willing to admit Shakespeare must have had "Latin enough to grammaticise his English". Alexander Pope, in his *Preface to the Works of Shakespeare*, knowing well enough that there was "certainly a vast difference between *learning* and *languages*", thought that it was "plain that he had much reading".

Steevens and Malone, after laborious research, took on the task of putting together a list of the translations of ancient authors into English that were known to have existed in the time of Shakespeare, as the source of all his classical erudition. That list falls far short of providing a satisfactory explanation of the matter, however. Especially in the face of numerous instances where such translations into English did *not* exist, it defies reality as much as the similar claim on behalf of the play "Timon of Athens", which, on investigation, turns out to have been founded in great part upon the *untranslated* Greek of Lucian.

In addition to all that, it has now been established by modern scholars that Shakespeare drew materials, ideas and even expressions from the Greek tragedies of Sophocles and Euripides, and even from Plato's works, and also from the Latin of Ovid, Virgil, Horace, Seneca and Tacitus, not to mention numerous others of the ancient classics, and apparently with the utmost indifference to the question of whether they had ever been translated into English or not.

Indeed, his learning covered the widest range. The notably controversial author on Shakespeare, John Payne Collier, profoundly impressed by a certain frequency of legal terms and expressions in the plays, went so far, on discovering this, as to add an entire new passage to his existing biography of William Shakespeare, to the effect that, in his youth, he had studied law in the office of an attorney, or, at least, of a bailiff, at Stratford. Moreover Lord Chief Justice Campbell, in his learned essay of addressed to him upon the subject, *Shakespeare's Legal Acquirements*, comes to the following conclusion upon Shakespeare's juridical phrases and forensic allusions:

"I am amazed not only by their number, but by the accuracy and propriety with which they are uniformly introduced."

It is clear from what we have just been learning from a topflight lawyer that William Shakespeare must have been deeply experienced in matters relating to the legal profession.

Chapter 2
Biographical without doubt.

The time has now come to put down, as completely as can reasonably be done, all that is known *for certain* about the man officially, and most widely, held to have been responsible for the literary output of the man known to *us* as William Shakespeare of Stratford-upon-Avon *and to his contemporaries* as William Shaksper, also of Stratford-upon-Avon.

The following is a summary of what is for the most part on record and, where it is not, is generally agreed. There will of course be occasional repetitions of what has been said earlier in this book, but it must be as well, on something so fundamental to the subject-matter of this book, to have a reasonably comprehensive summary in one place.

According to the Stratford church's register, a boy who at the same time was given the name "Gulielmus filius Johannes Shakspere" (meaning "William son of John Shakespere") was baptised on the 26th of April 1564. The entry was recorded in Latin because, even in the Protestant England of that time, Latin was still in normal use in Church matters. This William was the third of eight children, *none* of the others of whom could read or write.

Of his childhood, literally nothing is known. All that anyone can do is to speculate. This of course, inevitably, is what has been done by his biographers, all of them, even though, very obviously, on such a subject speculation is valueless. Even of the schooling, if any, that was part of his early life, nothing is known from anything recorded by anyone or by any institution.

In particular, there are no records of any sort of his even having *attended* the local grammar school at Stratford, let alone of his having impressed local contemporaries with his intelligence and wide learning. Even after he became famous nationwide, none of the teachers at that school put on record anything about the budding genius that the future William Shakespeare must, surely, have very evidently been.

Legend, of which, however, as far as anything recorded in writing is concerned, was non-existent until well after his death, has it that at the age of thirteen he was apprenticed to his father as a butcher and a glover, a glover being someone who makes gloves – perhaps out of the hides of the animals that were butchered?

In November 1582, at the age of eighteen, he married Anne Hathaway, who was already pregnant with their first child. This child, Susanna, was born six months later, during the following May, in 1583.

In 1585, a boy and a girl, the twins Hamnet and Judith, were born into the family. Surely rather strangely, those names given to them were the names of their neighbours, Hamnet and Judith Sadler.

To the best of our knowledge, the three Shakspere children were never taught to read or write.

Susanna and Judith both lived to quite an advanced old age.

After the birth of the twins there is silence until an event in 1592 in which one of the parties involved *may* have been him – we cannot be completely certain. What is on record is that in London during that year a "Willelmus Shackspere" – note the inconsistency of the spelling if it is the same person – made a loan of £7 to one John Clayton.

Three years later, in March 1595, "William Shakespeare", this time thus spelt, together with William Kempe and Richard Burbage, "servants to the Lord Chamberlain," received £20 for theatrical performances at the Royal court, in London, that had taken place during the previous December. Whether this William Shakespeare was the same person as the "Willelmus Shackspere" who lent £7 to someone called to John Clayton is something that we cannot know or even confidently presume.

In the following year in 1596, Hamnet, the only son of William and his wife Anne, died in Stratford at the age of eleven.

In 1597, and again in 1598 and 1599, "William Shackspere", this time thus spelt, is listed as a tax defaulter in Bishopsgate in London. It is possible that this offence occurred because, as we are about to learn, William Shackspere was no longer in London, having moved back to Stratford.

Yes, in 1597 he was living in Stratford, and, what is more, in dramatically improved financial circumstances. It is on record that during that year "Willielmin Shakespeare" purchased New Place, a large property in Stratford, and that he also made an application for a coat of arms, an extraordinary improvement in his situation, and all the more so given that acting was by no means a highly-paid profession.

From 1599 to 1608, various documents record the involvement of William Shakespeare with the Globe theatre in London, both as a shareholder and as a member of the King's Men.

From 1596 to 1616 most of what is on record during those twenty years places William Shakspere as a landowner and as a dealer in "bagged commodities" – which particular commodities is not specified – in Stratford. During that period of some twenty years he was also a litigant in several lawsuits to recover minor debts.

In April 1616 he died. Astonishingly by any yardstick, let alone if he was the deeply learned and highly successful author William Shakespeare who has been such a dominating literary force ever since, no books or manuscripts of any kind were listed in his will. That would have been an anomaly for *any* educated man of that time, when books were rare and valuable, and especially so by comparison with the ready availability books today.

Even more astonishingly, his death went unremarked by *anyone*. (By contrast, it is for instance on record that, when the Shakespearean actor Richard Burbage died in 1619, the whole of London went in mourning.)

From 1616 until the present day, no letters, no diaries, no memoranda, no documents of any kind that look as though they might have been hand-written by William Shakspere have ever come to light. The grand total that survives of what he ever wrote, or even *might* have written, consists of just six signatures, three of which are the signatures to his will, and in each of which his name is spelt differently from how it is spelt in the other five signatures.

Not only that, but, as the award-winning novelist Maggie O'Farrell – whose recent novel, *Hamnet*, is about the Shaksper son who died at the age of eleven – justifiably complained (as recorded in *The Times* newspaper of 26th May 2020):

> What really gets me going is that none of the people who must have known Shakespeare thought of going to Stratford after his death in 1616 and saying to Judith, by then over seventy, and to Susanna, aged sixty-seven:
>
>> "What was your father like? Tell us about him. What was he like to live with? What did he eat for breakfast?"
>
> Think about the value of the information those two could have contributed to what we know about him. But it is gone, and of course there are no direct descendants."

Quite so, Miss O'Farrell.

The foregoing, ladies and gentlemen, is *the total documented life* of the man who (a) is believed by many to be the greatest writer in the English language, and one of the greatest writers in any language, (b) added more than three thousand words to our vocabulary, and (c) dramatically changed the world of literature for ever.

Yes, this person, who as far as records are concerned, was almost non-existent, is supposed to have written, from 1593 onwards and starting at the age of twenty-nine, dramas that are about as sophisticated in every relevant way as anything ever written – dramas, moreover, that included features that make it impossible that William Shakespeare could be the William Shaksper of Stratford. In the first place, having spent his life only in Stratford and in London, he could not possibly have had any personal experience of them. In the second place, no other source of knowledge about them could have been available to him.

The features just referred to embraced:

– Effortless competence in classical Latin and Greek and in contemporary French, including the colloquial French and Italian of that time.

– Acquaintance with certain parts of Europe and their cultures that only someone who had visited them could have had.

– A knowledge of court life, including court manners, that only people who were part of the world of monarchs, their families and their courtiers could have had.

– A knowledge of English law that only a highly experienced practising lawyer could have.

– The fine arts.

– Music, medicine and heraldry.

– Knowledge of such pastimes as stag-hunting, falconry, bowls and royal tennis that belonged to the upper levels of the society of that time.

I rest this part of my case.

Chapter 3
Opening the question:
Who, then, *was* "William Shakespeare"?

Of some interest, especially to those who are at least wavering in their conviction that William Shakespeare was William Shaksper of Stratford-upon-Avon, are the following:

– The first of Shakespeare's plays to become publicly available, before the appearance of the 1623 First Folio, were published either anonymously or under the name "William Shake-Speare" – a name clearly expected to be recognised as a pseudonym – on the title page.

– There was no sort of official indication that the Stratford William Shakspere was the author until well over a century later, in 1769, when the famous actor David Garrick launched enthusiastic public celebrations on the banks of the River Avon.

– *Not until as late as the middle of the 19th century* was there any attempt to give a coherent explanation to show how it could be possible that this person and the astonishing, well-educated genius who is responsible for the works of Shakespeare could be the same person.

With that background in place let us now return to the thirteen questions that I put in front of my readers in Chapter 1 of this PART II.

Out of most of those questions even a single one of them, just by itself, together with the fact that to none of them has any credible answer has ever been given, would be enough to rule out any possibility that the Will Shaksper of Stratford that we have just been learning about could have been the author of the works of William Shakespeare. And I assert this as someone fortunate enough to possess a massive collection of works of every kind on Shakespeare and related matters and to have had discussions on the subject with very many people over the years. All the more so, of course, does this "non-answerability" apply to *all thirteen* of those unanswerable questions.

This, moreover, is so *plainly* the case that I invite all the academics and other experts on Shakespeare, and of course the "ordinary folk" among my readers as well, to consider themselves firmly confronted with this assertion of mine: that Shaksper *cannot* be Shakespeare. The notion that he could be Shakespeare is actually, and without exaggeration, an absurdity. I even go so far as to suggest that any readers who do not face up to that clear reality are being intellectually defiant, and that is putting it politely.

The question therefore now arises: who, then, might this extraordinary person, evidently of both extraordinary genius and deep learning, have been?

*   *   *   *   *

Not surprisingly, given the surely-clear *impossibility* that Stratford's Will Shaksper could be the author of some of the most important works of literature ever composed, great efforts have been made by many people to identify the real author. Indeed the search has continued, unabated, right up to our present day.

I do not exaggerate when I say that the results of all this scholarly activity have been startling. With the help of the Internet I have located more than *eighty* people, including the occasional lady, on behalf of whom one or more serious claims have been made that the person in question is the *true* "William Shakespeare". If only to have it set down in hard print, I shall now give a list of those of which I am aware.

I cannot, of course, offer any guarantee that the list is complete even at the time that I am writing these words. Nor – and even less so – can I guarantee that it will remain as complete as it is now for any significant length of time in the future.

Simply to make what follows as un-daunting to the reader as I reasonably can, I have divided the contenders into three groups.

The first group is those who over the years have had the widest support for claims on their behalf for the authorship, in approximate order of the amount of support enjoyed by each of them.

The second group consists of those with titles of nobility or higher, arranged in order of the social status of the various titles in including ecclesiastical titles. This particular list, in addition to being convenient in that it creates another grouping, is reasonably logical for this purpose because royalty and noblemen abound in the plays.

The third group consists of all the other people on behalf of whom the claim has been made, with their names arranged in alphabetical order.

Very occasionally names belong to, and appear in, more than one of the three groups.

I have added dates of birth and / or death where either or both of these are known, and also the occupation, if any, for which that person is best known.

If any readers wish to give these lists, and especially the last one, only cursory attention, I shall have no objection. My reason for providing them is mainly that I think it worth having the lists on record.

Group number one. Those with widest support.

Sir Francis Bacon (1561–1626), lawyer, at one time Attorney General and at another time Lord Chancellor, scholarly writer and essayist.

Edward de Vere, the 17th Earl of Oxford (1550-1604), a courtier, a poet and a playwright.

Christopher Marlowe (1564-1593).

William Stanley, the 6th Earl of Derby (1561-1642).

Sir Walter Raleigh (1552-1618).

John Donne (1572-1681).

Group number two. Those with titles of nobility or higher, but excluding knights – all arranged in order of the social status of the titles.

Queen Elizabeth I (1533–1603), Queen of England, known as "The Virgin Queen".

King Edward VI (1537–1553), King of England.

King James VI of Scotland, later also King James I of England (1566–1625).

Queen Mary, Mary Queen of Scots (1542–1587).

William Alexander, 1st Earl of Stirling (1568–1640).

Lancelot Andrewes, Bishop of Winchester (1555–1626).

Charles Blount, (1563–1606), 8th Baron Mountjoy and 1st Earl of Devonshire, and Knight of the Garter.

The Rev. Miles Bodley (dates not known for certain but thought to be 1553–1611), a Bible scholar.

Robert Cecil (1563–1612), 1st Earl of Salisbury, a notable statesman.

Thomas Cecil (1542-1623), 1st Earl of Exeter, a soldier and a notable politician.

Walter Devereux, 1st Earl of Essex (1541?–1576), possibly in partnership with his son Robert (see below).

Robert Devereux, 2nd Earl of Essex (1566–1601).

Fulke Greville (1554–1628), 1st Baron Brooke.

The Jesuits as a group. This was proposed by Harold Johnson in 1916 in his book *Did the Jesuits Write "Shakespeare"?*.

William Stanley, 6th Earl of Derby (1561–1642).

Gilbert Talbot 7th Earl of Shrewsbury (1552–1616).

William Warner (c. 1558–1609), a poet.

Group number three. The remainder – starting with knights, in alphabetical order, and following them with all the others, again in alphabetical order.

Anthony Bacon (1558–1601), a statesman.

John Barnard (1604–1674), husband, at least supposedly, of Shaksper's granddaughter.

Barnabe Barnes (1571–1609), a poet and playwright.

Richard Barnfield (1574–1620) a poet.

Sir Thomas Bodley (1545–1613), a diplomat.

Richard Burbage (1567–1619), an actor.

Robert Burton (1577–1640), known only as a scholar.

William Butts (date of birth unknown approximately 1486, died 1583), a member of King Henry VIII's court and King Henry's physician, and a patron of literature.

Edmund Campion (1540–1581), a Jesuit priest who was arrested by priest hunters, convicted of high treason because of his Catholic practices, and hanged, drawn and quartered at Tyburn Tree, which was where London's Marble Arch is now situated.

Miguel de Cervantes (1547–1616), the Spanish novelist, poet and playwright famed for being the supposed – but not necessarily actual – author of the world's first novel, *The Ingenious Gentleman Don Quixote of La Mancha*.

Henry Chettle (1560–1607), a playwright.

Michelangelo Crollalanza (1564 to date-of-death-unknown). Little is known about him but he is thought to have been born in Sicily.

Samuel Daniel, (1562–1619), both a poet and a historian.

Daniel Defoe (1660–1731), famous as the author of the novel *Robinson Crusoe*.

Edward de Vere (1550–1604), the 17th Earl of Oxford, a courtier, a poet and a playwright.

Thomas Dekker (1572–1632), a playwright.

Leonard Digges (c.1515–c.1559), a scientist.

John Donne, (1572–1631,) Dean of St. Paul's Cathedral and a poet.

Sir Francis Drake (1540–1596), famous as both a naval commander and a sea-adventurer.

Michael Drayton (1563–1631), a playwright.

Sir Edward Dyer, (1543–1607), a courtier and a poet.

Henry Ferrers (1549–1633), a Member of Parliament and an antiquary.

John Fletcher (1579–1625), a playwright.

John Florio (1554–1625), an author and teacher (mainly of languages).

Michelangelo Florio (1515–1572), also known as "Crollalanza", a scholarly Protestant evangelist.

Stephen Gosson (1554-1624), the author of the work titled *The Schoole of Abuse, containing a pleasant invective against Poets, Pipers, Plaiers, Jesters and such like Caterpillars of the Commonwealth* (1579), and also of a few pamphlets.

Robert Greene (1558–1592), a popular dramatist and pamphleteer of his day, known for his negative critiques of his colleagues and for a pamphlet published after his death, *Greene's Groats-Worth of Witte, bought with a million of Repentance*, that was actually thought by many to include an attack on Shakespeare.

Bartholomew Griffin (date of birth unknown, died 1602), a poet.

Anne Hathaway, (1556–1623), the wife of William Shaksper.

William Herbert (1580–1630), the 3rd Earl of Pembroke, a scholar who was Chancellor of the University of Oxford and the founder Oxford's Pembroke College.

Thomas Heywood, (1574–1641), a playwright.

Ben Jonson (1572–1637), a playwright and a poet.

Thomas Kyd (1558–1594), a playwright.

Emilia Lanier (1569–1645), originally Emilia Bassano, a poet.

Thomas Lodge (1557–1625), a playwright.

John Lyly (1554–1606), a playwright and a theatre troupe manager.

Elizabeth Sidney Manners (1585-1612), Countess of Rutland, the only surviving child of Sir Phillip Sidney, who was both a military hero and a poet.

Roger Manners, 5th Earl of Rutland (1576–1612).

Sir Tobie Matthew (1577–1655), a Catholic priest and a courtier.

Thomas Middleton (1580–1627), a playwright.

Saint and Sir Thomas More (1478–1535), Lord Chancellor of England and a canonised Catholic saint.

Anthony Munday (1560–1633), a playwright.

Thomas Nashe (1567–1601), a playwright, a poet, a satirist and a pamphleteer.

Henry Neville (1564–1615), a courtier and a politician.

Sir Thomas North (1535–1604), a justice of the peace, a military officer and a translator who most notably translated into English Plutarch's *Lives of the Noble Greeks and Romans*, which was used as a source text by William Shakespeare for the plays *Julius Caesar*, *Coriolanus* and *Antony and Cleopatra*.

William Nugent (1550–1625), Irish rebel against the régime of King Henry VIII.

Henry Paget (1539-1568), 2nd Baron Paget, an English Member of Parliament as well as a peer.

George Peele (1556–1596), a playwright.

William Pierce (1561–1674), a now-unknown author.

Henry Porter (1596–99), a playwright.

The famous historical figure, Sir Walter Raleigh (1554–1618).

Thomas Sackville, Lord Buckhurst, and then the 1st Earl of Dorset (1536–1608).

William Seymour, a "bastardised" son of Earl of Hertford and Lady Catherine Grey, and supposedly raised by Mary Shakespeare.

Sir Anthony Shirley (1565?–1635), an aggressive soldier, sailor and adventurer, who conducted a number of overseas expeditions.

Mary Sidney Herbert (1561–1621), Countess of Pembroke.

Sir Philip Sidney (1554–1586), a courtier, a soldier and a poet.

Wentworth Smith (1571– c. 1623), a playwright.

Edmund Spenser (1552–1599), a lastingly famous poet, believed to have written, amongst other works, *The Faerie Queene,* an epic poem and allegory celebrating the Tudor dynasty and Elizabeth I.

Perhaps the most remarkable feature of all in the names listed above, indeed a genuinely astonishing one, is that they include no fewer than *four* British monarchs. That is not unfitting given that as many as ten of the Shakespeare plays, approximately a quarter of them, are centred on monarchs and have in their title a monarch's name; but even so... I have thought it very much worth drawing attention to this feature, for a reason that will start to become clear in the next chapter.

*   *   *   *   *

If there were no readily available alternative, we might need to examine one by one the case for each of those claimed above. The amount of work needed in order to do this adequately would be dauntingly large; but of course it would be less so, both for me and for my readers, and possibly *very* much less so, if it were to turn out that we succeeded in reaching certainty as to who the author is – and I do mean *certainty,* rather than something in the region of *greatest probability* – before we had finished our journey through the list. Let hope, therefore, that it does indeed turn out so!

Where to start?

As logical place as any, surely, is with the candidate for the authorship who has had most support over the centuries. This is undoubtedly the author and politician who lived during the reigns of Queen Elizabeth I and King James VI of Scotland and I of England, who featured prominently in the history of the time, and who, after starting his adult life as Mr. Francis Bacon, went on to become Sir Francis Bacon and then the first Viscount St. Albans (*not* Viscount St. Alban, as he is often called).

If we do not find that we can arrive with absolute *certainty* at the conclusion that he was the author of the works attributed to William Shakespeare, we shall then move on to the second person on our list of possibilities, Edward de Vere, Earl of Oxford; and then, if we are still without a definite answer, to the third person; and so on, until we arrive at what is an evidently satisfactory answer – *if*, as I maintain we shall, we ever do arrive there.

Chapter 4
Starting with the most prominent of the leading candidates
for recognition as the true author.

"Prisoner in the dock, Sir Francis Bacon, Lord St. Albans: you stand accused of having written the execrable plays and other deplorable writings commonly attributed to William Shakespeare. Do you plead guilty or not guilty to the charge?"

No answer, of course. We shall have to proceed without the help of his direct co-operation.

*　　*　　*　　*　　*

By whatever kind of measuring-rod that anyone might think appropriate for such a purpose, Francis Bacon was a towering figure of his time. What is more, and unrecognised by most people, he is still wielding considerable influence today.

– He was a statesman – at different times Attorney General and, the highest political position under the monarchy in those days, Lord Chancellor. For a time, he ran the country jointly with King James I, who was his only superior in authority; and at one stage he was even *ruling* the country, as Regent.

– He was an influential philosopher, and was responsible for two massive philosophical works written by him in Latin: *Novum Organum Scientiarum*, which means "New Instrument *or* Method of Scientific Knowledge" and *De Augmentis Scientiarum*, which means "On the Advancement of Learning" and is also the title of an earlier and shorter version of that second book, written in English.

"Influential philosopher" is no exaggeration, incidentally. He is still recognised by many philosophers as the actual *founder* of the modern philosophy that has replaced the philosophy of Aristotle and St. Thomas Aquinas that had ruled Christendom from the 13th century until his day and continued to rule it for some time afterwards.

– He was a scientist, and is recognised as the father of what is called "The Scientific Method", which is a method of scientific enquiry (a) based on measurable evidence and (b) made subject to particular principles of reasoning.

– He was, and still is, a widely-read author, whose *Essays, or Counsels Civil and Moral*, for instance, are still in print in several editions today; and some critics have rated him as the greatest essayist of all, superior even to Montaigne and Samuel Johnson.

– He was a leading lawyer. Indeed it could be claimed that he was a *great* lawyer, for instance since he is acknowledged as the inventor of an important element of the Common Law as it is today: the process of discovering unwritten laws from the evidences of how they have been applied in the past.

For this reason, he is commemorated with a statue in Gray's Inn in central London, one of London's four *Inns of Court* (professional associations for barristers and judges) to which a person must belong in London in order to be "called to the bar" and to practise as a barrister in England and Wales.

At one stage he was Treasurer of Gray's Inn.

– He even played a leading role in establishing the British colonies in North America, especially those of Virginia, which originally stretched all the way from Florida in the south of

North America to Nova Scotia in Canada, and of North and South Carolina, and of Newfoundland in the north east of Canada, and that were the start of the biggest empire that has ever existed. Because of the considerable significance of this as a fundamental part of English history, I think it worth quoting this relevant passage in chapter 47 of *Sir Francis Bacon – A Biography* by Jean Overton Fuller (East West Publications 1981; revised edition George Mann of Maidstone, 1994):

In the Charter of Virginia Company of London of 23rd May 1609 there is a complete list of the shareholders. These include investors from various walks of life: noblemen and commoners, sailors and clansmen, the Earl of Montgomerie, the Earl of Pembroke, the Earl of Salisbury, the Earl of Southampton, Sir Francis Bacon Kt., Capt John Smith...

The document does not specify the sums invested by each one, and granted to them "in form hereafter in these presents expressed, whether they go in their persons to be planted there in the said plantation or whether they go not but do adventure their moneys, goods and chattels... that they themselves should be one body or perpetual community... and... should be known, called and incorporated by the name The Treasurer and Company of Adventurers and Planters of the City of London for the First Colony in Virginia."

The which company was granted a patent of rights.

There had been an earlier charter but we do not know what names were connected with it. Bacon had had one known earlier "adventure" in the New World. In 1607 he had been one of the founders of the Newfoundland Company, a short-lived as not very successful company for establishing a fishing colony in Newfoundland.

Now, he was one of the founders of the Virginia Company.

*   *   *   *   *

Whether the influence of Francis Bacon has been beneficial to the human race or harmful to it, which is a subject that we shall be looking at a little later in this book, the totality of the foregoing is a truly astonishing catalogue of accomplishment.

What is more, impressive though all that is, both in each individual item and in the accumulation of all of them, there is more, much more, to come; and I invite my readers, as they accompany me further, to do so in a spirit of excited anticipation.

Chapter 5
Enter ciphering and de-ciphering.

In Elizabethan England, an enthusiasm for ciphers – word-ciphers, anagrams, acrostics, and other kinds of ciphers – suddenly sprang into existence. That this should have happened is understandable. Terrifying persecutions in England, during the period of the religious revolution now known as the Reformation, had started with the first of the Tudor monarchs, King Henry VII, and one result of them had been a constant need for concealment by those who wanted to communicate anything controversial, particularly in religious matters.

After King Henry VII's reign had come to an end, such persecutions were be no means abandoned, other than – as most historians of the period do not recognise – during the reign of Queen Mary. From time to time, they were even greatly intensified; and one result was that the writing of secret messages in cipher – hidden in such places as the texts of manuscripts and books and even in places such as on gravestones – started up, became increasingly common, and eventually developed a life of its own.

One of the ciphers of that period was invented by Francis Bacon. We know this, and much about it, because he described it in considerable detail in his *De Augmentis Scientiarum* ("The Advancement of Learning"), the second of his two philosophical works. I now give a brief outline of what he says about his cipher in this book.

I owe no apology if what now follows, relating to the cipher concocted by Bacon, makes any of my readers' heads swim. It is necessary to give it because it is definitely relevant to our consideration of Francis Bacon as the possible "Shakespeare"; and it is, unfortunately, *intrinsically* complex.

In summary: –

– Enciphering a piece of prose in this instance involved using a concealed alphabet.

– This particular alphabet was constructed by

(a) using only the first two letters of the ordinary alphabet, A and B,

and

(b) writing them in varying shapes.

– Each A or B, whenever it appeared in the piece of prose in which ciphering had been included, would *also* represent *another* letter of the alphabet, in accordance with whatever its shape was.

– But, in any document enciphered in this way, the letters A and B, strangely-constructed – in italics of various shapes – for no evidently good reason, would appear in sentences that gave o*rdinary* messages that the writer was happy for anyone to read, *while also*, secretly, representing *different* letters.

– These different letters, when taken together in the order in which they appeared, would form words that were otherwise hidden.

– These hidden words, again when taken together in the order in which they appeared, would create a secret sentence.

One other background fact: Bacon made it clear that this was only one of several ciphers that he used for concealed messages.

What he did *not* do, either in *De Augmentis Scientiarum* or anywhere else in his writings, was to say where, if anywhere, he used this or any other cipher. This omission was clearly deliberate. Understandably, he did not want his enciphered messages to reach people that he wished to conceal those messages from.

In our present day, however, we have an advantage that his contemporaries did not have and which I shall now present to my gracious readers.

In 1893, there entered into the public arena in the United States the first volume of what would end up being a work of five volumes, written by an until-then completely unknown author, Dr. Orville Ward Owen, whose career up to that point in his life had been that of professional physician. It was titled *Sir Francis Bacon's Cipher Story* and it eventually consisted of, in total, a thousand and one pages of poetry that, in both its content and its manner and style of composition, clearly resembled authentic Shakespearean verse. Here are the first few lines of a lengthy piece of verse in it titled "Description of the Queen, General Curse, and Sir Francis Bacon's Life":

SWEET SIR

Lo! Here led by eternal Providence
To succour me from out this cloudy vale,
And having fortune, fate and heavenly destiny obeyed,
As fortune friends the bold, now will I
Reveal to happy prey to you
Who makes great fortune's wheel turn as you please;...

What Dr. Owen's five-volume compilation was "all about" is conveniently summarised in a collection of articles, in a periodical, the *Detroit Journal* (of Detroit, Michigan), that had been provoked in response to a shorter version of the contents of the first volume that Dr. Owen had published a little earlier, and which he now included at the end of this volume because of the articles' obvious interest – indeed, more than mere interest, even *importance* in relation to such a controversial matter.

I shall now reproduce some highlights from those *Detroit Journal* articles that were reproduced at the end of Dr. Owen's first volume.

The first of these articles, which appeared in the *Detroit Journal* of 14th September 1893, was by a Mr. George P. Goodale, the dramatic critic of the *Detroit Journal*. Headed "Shakespeare-Bacon", it proceeded:

For many years the tide of talk connecting the name of Francis Bacon with the authorship of the Shakespeare plays has flowed and ebbed. The Baconians, being the accusers, have had to assume the burden of proof. They have been flouted, scorned and pooh-poohed with pitying and often supercilious superiority by those who insist that William Shakespeare, of Stratford, wrote the plays that are ascribed to him.

Shakespeare was for me too dear and too real a friend to be easily thrown overboard. I now, however, find myself forced to the conviction that Francis Bacon wrote the Shakespeare plays, a conviction that is the result of more than a year's examination of testimony submitted to me by Dr. Orville W. Owen of Detroit, a tireless gentleman who not only discovered the hidden cipher but has worked out the secret stories hidden by it.

In July, 1892, Dr. Owen confided to me the cipher, and together we went over the matter which is contained in the volume now being published by him. I was shown how to apply the cipher for the unfolding of these startling revelations. Crucially, *I saw that there was nothing of conjecture in it*, but a simple, unerring mechanical process.

At first, and with amazement obscuring my judgement, I found it impossible to admit what *now* appears to me to the clearest truth. This radical uprooting of all my life's ideas on the momentous issue of the authorship of the works of Shakespeare cost me much. If ever I saw duty confronting me, however, I see it now. I feel, in simplest honour, bound to make proclamation that, as far as I am concerned, the evidence offered by Dr. Owen is overwhelming.

I realise that my conclusions may not move a single mind to change; but, with whatever result, I believe that what now follows needs to be said.

1. Dr. Orville W. Owen, of Detroit, Michigan, U. S. A., is the actual and sole discoverer of a practical scheme of cipher writing in which, when what is enciphered is deciphered, it can be seen to be asserted that:

(a) Francis Bacon was the lawful son of Elizabeth. Queen of England, and Robert Dudley, the Earl of Leicester, those two having been secretly married in the Tower of London.

What? Wh...a...t? I *beg* your pardon. *What* did Mr. Goodale say? Did he *really* say what I have just represented him as saying jointly with Dr. Owen? Did he *really* say that the works of

William Shakespeare were written by the *son*, and the *legitimate* son, of Queen Elizabeth I – who, for Heaven's sake, known in her lifetime and throughout subsequent history as "The *Virgin Queen*" – from which it follows that, rightfully, Francis Bacon was eligible to be *the King of England* – King Francis I – when she died?

After pausing briefly for an astonished gulp, I continue with Mr. Goodale.

> (b) That Francis Bacon, for the purpose of concealing the secret histories which he wrote "for posterity," composed the following:
>
> > all the plays of Shakespeare, Christopher Marlow, Robert Green and George Peele;
> >
> > *The Anatomy of Melancholy* of Robert Burton, and all the works of Edmund Spenser.
>
> These, taken in connection with the undisputed works of Bacon, constitute the general fabric into which are woven the threads that form the cypher stories.
>
> 2. Dr. Owen has worked out by a process known to me (and of which any man who so wills may inform himself) various stories, every line of which is taken systematically from the works enumerated in the foregoing paragraph. The first of these secret stories is entitled, "The Letter to the Decipherer". The third and largest (unfinished) division of the book comprises a description of Queen Elizabeth; an extraordinary composition called *The General Curse*; and Bacon's *Autobiography*.

For my part I could wish that this whole revelation were a dream, and that our immortal Shakespeare's crown were not in dispute. He would for ever be my friend who would settle the controversy in favour of Shakespeare. Meanwhile, however, there are three things in particular to be take definite note of:

> 1. The existence of a cipher by use of which these stories are revealed is an indisputable fact.

2. The stories are not Dr. Owen's inventions. He did not compose them, for the reason that neither he nor any man that lives is gifted with the surpassing genius that would be needed to do this.

3. Nobody has the right to pass judgment on this discovery who has not first read Dr. Owen's book, *Sir Francis Bacon's Cipher Story*.

What follows now is from another article from the *Detroit Journal*, this one by its Managing Editor, Mr. W. J. Hunsaker.

The natural question that will force itself upon the mind of the reader of this remarkable book is:

Has Dr. Owen really discovered a cipher story in the works, or has he laboriously pieced out, with most cunning ingenuity, a story that, in, its relations to history, bears close resemblance to reality?

Or has he only concocted a clever imposture, written a story shrewdly calculated to find dupes in those who have a leaning toward the Baconian side of the ancient controversy over the authorship of those immortal plays that for centuries have borne the name of William Shakespeare?

It may be stated, in the first place, that this is Dr. Owen's first venture in the field of letters and that he is a man who has reached middle age; that he has never shown the slightest sign of possessing unusual or extraordinary literary skill or genius; that the story is written in a style that shows great facility in the so-called Shakespearean blank verse; and that the story itself is a production betraying, on almost every page, the hand of an author of broad learning, deep thought, intense poetical feeling, and wide range of intellect.

Important, obviously, is this point, upon which Dr. Owen lays stress:

If Bacon did not write the cipher story, then Dr. Owen did, and, for whatever merit there is in it, Dr. Owen should have the credit. It will be conceded that the story is a remarkable production, and, this conceded, it then remains to take the horns of this dilemma:

110

either the story is true,

or Dr. Owen is a charlatan, but also the most wonderful man who has lived since the beginning of the seventeenth century.

We believe that most readers, personally unacquainted with the author, will find it difficult to reach a verdict. They will be stunned with the marvel of it, and still be fortified with the generally diffused dislike to acknowledge that an iconoclast is right. The history is by no means finished with this volume, but it is to be continued in another book, as also shall follow the exposition of the cipher itself.

When these further volumes appear, it will be the preponderating sentiment, perhaps, that in *Sir Francis Bacon's Cipher Story* Dr. Owen has given to the world a most astounding production.

Also relevant, for a reason that will very soon emerge, is this extract from Dr. Owen's Preface at the beginning of the fifth and final volume.

In Book III of *The Cipher Story*, I took pleasure in acknowledging the aid of my assistants in the preparation of that volume. Their work had by then demonstrated that the correct use of the Cipher could be acquired by others.

The present volume, Book V, is entirely their work. Miss Ollie E. Wheeler extracted from the original Shakespeare Plays, from Bacon's acknowledged works, and from those attributed to Marlowe, Greene, Peele, Spenser and Burton, the passages around the guides and numerous keys. Mrs. Elizabeth W. Gallup and Miss Kate E. Wells, have deciphered and woven these passages, by the rules of the Cipher, into the poetic form in which they are presented.

I congratulate my assistants upon their work, and the world upon this unanswerable proof of the certainty of the Cipher system.

What, for our purposes, is the relevance of that? It is the mention and naming there of one of his assistants, Mrs. Gallup, with whom I am now going to make my readers more closely acquainted.

Chapter 6
Mrs. Gallup: can we justifiably believe
what she has to tell us?

Mrs. Elizabeth Wells Gallup (her full name), was, like Dr. Owen, a citizen of the United States of America, where she mainly lived during her lifetime of 1848 to 1934. As we are about to see, she was far from being merely a valued assistant to Dr. Owen. In her own right, she can fairly be described as, by any standards, a truly remarkable lady.

Exceptionally intelligent and learned, she continued independently the research that she had been helping Dr. Owen with, and, by dint of heroic labour, eventually succeeded in becoming the leading expert in the world on what is known as the Baconian or bi-literal cipher – clearly a subject of some importance, given that, if someone takes great trouble taken to conceal something, he is, obviously, likely to have taken that trouble for what he considers to be good reason.

She ended up completing a classic treatment of the subject, titled by her *The Bi-literal Cypher of Sir Francis Bacon Discovered in his Works and Deciphered*, published in 1899.

Here is what Mrs. Gallup, after bringing to notice various books written by Bacon, tells her readers in the very first page of her book:

> Students of these old editions have been impressed with the extraordinary number of words and passages, often unimportant, printed in italics, where no known rule of construction would require the use of italics. There has been no reasonable explanation on this until now, when it has been found that they were so used for the purpose of this Cipher.

Having become satisfied, from examining original editions of Bacon's works, that there were hidden messages in at least some of them, she pursued the nightmarishly demanding task of decoding such messages as she succeeded in finding. Intrigued, too, when she learnt that, a few decades earlier, in 1848, some scholars in England had started to maintain that the works of Shakespeare were written, not by the William Shakespeare of Stratford, but by Francis Bacon, she took it upon herself to examine the original editions of some of Shakespeare's writings as well.

What she came up with was startling beyond any realistic possibility of exaggeration. So much so, indeed, that, before I outline it, I believe I ought to show, as can easily be done, that no one could reasonably think Mrs. Gallup to be anything other than worthy of respect, as a scholarly, conscientious and sober-minded lady.

By the time her formal education had finally come to an end, Mrs. Gallup had studied in three universities: Eastern Michigan University in the United States, the Sorbonne in Paris, and the University of Marburg in Germany. She had also been a school's headmistress for some twenty years. There is thus no reason whatever to question either her competence or her sincerity. In fact even the care and the amount of detail that evidently went into the construction of her book are sufficient to give ample evidence of both of those qualities.

Because of its obviously being desirable for to us make as good a judgment as we reasonably can as whether we can consider ourselves entitled to trust what Mrs. Gallup has to say as genuine, rather than an extraordinary fiction concocted by her, I think it worth quoting another author who made extensive use of her work, Mr. Parker Woodward, on the first page of his book, *Tudor Problems* (Gay and Hancock, London, 1912):

> Although Francis Bacon openly stated that he invented the bi-literal cipher when he was a young man in France, at that time associated with the British Embassy where cipher-writing of different kinds would be studied and practised, and although the cipher discovered by Mrs. Gallup may spell out a story, it is of course possible that she has not been truthful in her claim that the story really is the result of her deciphering, rather than a piece of fiction concocted by her. And not least because of the extent of the authorship claims that the

ciphered – or supposedly ciphered – story makes, there must be a duty to work out whether what is alleged in it is in fact true.

As to the *bona fides* of the decipherer, no one who has met the lady and seen her method of working could have any doubts on that score, and anyway she would have needed to possess a marvellous genius – indeed an "impossible" genius – to produce the story as told, and all the more so if the story is capable of being confirmed from other sources. In this chapter [of Parker Woodward's book] it is proposed to discuss whether historical facts do indeed confirm allegation that Queen Elizabeth and Lord Robert Dudley were married.

Against that background, I shall now give a summary of Mrs. Gallup's findings, occasionally supplemented with the findings of subsequent authors who, having read her book, succeeded in developing further what she had initiated. I invite you, gracious readers, as you are about to start reading what follows, to make a resolve to adhere wholeheartedly to certain principles that I have emphasised earlier in this book, and which are never more necessary to keep constantly in mind than they will be here, and for which, this time, I shall make use of the words of Mrs. Gallup herself as a reminder.

From page 4 of her same book:

I would beg that the readers of this book will bring to the consideration of this work minds that are free from prejudice, making their judgements of it with the same intelligence and impartiality they would themselves desire if the presentation were their own. Otherwise doing this work will, indeed, have been a thankless task for me.

Enlightened, good readers, if you should need to be, by those inspiring words, please prepare to be enthralled and captivated as you have seldom, if ever, been before. Take a deep breath in eager anticipation... – and...

No. Before I invite you to read on, I should like to make clear something that is of obvious importance, given what I can confidently foresee what the reaction of some people – and especially some people in the ranks of academia – is going to be in the face of what is coming next.

This that I emphasise that, although I shall be making quite extensive use of Mrs. Gallup's work, which I believe I am fully justified in doing, I shall not be using her as actually an *authority*, and I shall not be in any way relying on her for such a purpose. Rather, I shall be using her to open our eyes to possibilities that otherwise would not have occurred to us. That done, I shall then weigh up those possibilities *independently* of her.

In other words, this part of this book is very different from what it would have been if Mrs. Gallup had not engaged herself in her heroic labours, but the *responsibility* for the accuracy of whatever I put forward as fact, and indicate my belief that it should be accepted as fact, remains firmly with me.

I return now to where I broke off three paragraphs back. Please prepare to be enthralled and captivated as you have seldom, if ever, been before. Take a deep breath in eager anticipation... – and read on.

In 1554 Queen Elizabeth I, when she was still Princess Elizabeth, was, as we have already learned from Mr. George Goodale, imprisoned in the Tower of London, where, at the same time and for much the same reason, Lord Robert Dudley, brother-in-law of Lady Jane Grey, was also suffering imprisonment. There they fell in love *and were secretly married by a monk*. This marriage took place even though, shockingly, Dudley was *already* married. He was married to a young lady called Amy Robsart, who was the daughter – in fact the only legitimate child – of Sir John Robsart, Lord of the Manor of Syderstone Hall in Norfolk.

In 1560, by which time Princess Elizabeth had become Queen Elizabeth, and indeed had been Queen Elizabeth for two years, Amy Dudley, Lord Robert Dudley's by-then-inconvenient *real* wife, was killed at her home, allegedly by falling down a flight of stairs. It was suspected by many at the time that this unlikely event was *not* an accident, and that her husband was responsible for his wife's death.

In September of the same year, a *second* marriage between Elizabeth and Robert Dudley took place, again in secret as far as the general public was concerned (although, as the Spanish ambassador of that time reported to his King, King Philip, rumours of their relationship had been circulating all over the country), but this time in front of a sufficient number of witnesses to leave no doubt that the marriage had taken place if the Queen should ever want that known, and officially formalising her married state.

Four months later, in January 1561 according to Mrs. Gallup's findings, Queen Elizabeth secretly gave birth to a son, whom she named Francis, and who, thanks to her recent marriage, was of course her *legitimate* son, and indeed, as the eldest son of a monarch, officially entitled to be called the Prince of Wales – *and*, as noted earlier, in chapter 5, in due course King Francis I.

She persuaded one of her two leading officers of state, Sir Nicholas Bacon, the Lord Keeper of the Great Seal, and his wife, Lady (Anne) Bacon, who was one of her official Companions (a Companion being a member, male or female, of one of the grades of knighthood), to adopt him as their own child, thus becoming officially the youngest of their several children.

Francis Bacon did not learn of this, and that he was in reality potentially a future king, until fifteen years later, in 1576, when, in a fit of anger caused by Court gossip on the matter that she had become aware of, she admitted to Francis that she was his mother but added that she would never acknowledge him as such.

In 1567, on 10th November of that year according to the ciphered account, there was born to Queen Elizabeth and her secret husband Robert Dudley a second son, whom she named Robert. This son was given to her friend and cousin Lady Hereford, also the Queen's Mistress of the Robes, to be brought up by her and her husband. A little later, Queen Elizabeth gave Lord Hereford an estate in the county of Essex and a higher-ranking title, the Earldom of Essex, which young Robert inherited on Lord Hereford's death in 1576, thereby becoming himself the Earl of Essex.

Evidently she was determined to remain, in the *highest* degree hypocritically, "the Virgin Queen".

Throughout young Essex's life, the relationship between him and his *real* mother, Queen Elizabeth, was sometimes close, sometimes quarrelsome and sometimes even worse than merely quarrelsome. Shockingly, it ended with an attempted *coup d'état* by Essex, with the aim of, *in effect* removing the Queen from her office as the *actual* ruler of her realm, with him then governing in her name. The attempt failed, and in 1601 he was tried for high treason, convicted, sentenced to death, and beheaded.

So much for Essex.

Francis Bacon's life could hardly have been more different. The bare outline of it, from the time that he reached early adulthood, is a matter of public record, and the most important early event in it took place in 1576, when he accompanied the English ambassador, Amias Paulet, on a journey to France, and spent some two years there. According to the ciphered accounts that Mrs. Gallup made available to us, however, there is much that is *not* on public record and that was revealed in those accounts for the first time a century or so ago.

Recognised by many from early on as prodigy of intelligence and intellectual creativity, as the ciphered material clearly implies from time to time, Francis Bacon wholeheartedly embraced the profession of authorship. Much that he wrote he did not publish under his own name. He does not say why, but it is not difficult to think of possible reasons. One obvious one is that the name "Bacon", as I hope I may say without causing offence to any of my readers who happen to bear it, is not a particularly appealing name, and indeed we can imagine him pondering on the strange misfortune that had artificially imposed it on him and, at the same time, had made it impossible for him to use the name that he *ought* to have been entitled to.

Why impossible? Consider the implications that such recognition would have for his *real* mother.

In the first place she was, as already noted, publicly promoting herself as "the Virgin Queen". And, in the words of the cliché, you can say *that* again! – in that she was doing it even to the extent of her supposed virginity being commemorated in the very name, Virginia, of what is even today a large part of North America, nearly forty thousand square miles in area, and was originally well over sixty thousand square miles.

In the second place, and far more seriously, if it were to be learnt that she had married Robert Dudley, and for that reason had made him Earl of Leicester, in both cases almost immediately after the death of his wife Amy, no more would be needed to confirm in the public mind the long-running suspicion that, between them, she and Dudley had been responsible for Amy's death.

Certainly Queen Elizabeth took precautions, and with the utmost ruthlessness, to minimise the possibility of her relationship with Dudley being publicly aired. As we can read in the authoritative Oxford *Dictionary of National Biography* (originally published in 1882, and with supplements continually added until 1990), in volume xvi, page 114:

Whatever were the Queen's relations with Dudley before his wife's death, they became closer after. It was reported that she was formally betrothed to him and that she had secretly married him in Lord Pembroke house, and that she was a mother already.

In 1562 the report that Elizabeth had children by Dudley were revived. One, Robert Brooks of Devizes, was sent to prison for publishing the slander, and seven years later a man named Marsham, of Norwich, was punished for the same offence.

*   *   *   *   *

Before we return to the messages that Mrs. Gallup decoded, there is another general fact about Queen Elizabeth that is worth putting on record here. This is her relationship, often not mentioned by those who have written about her, with a certain Dr. John Dee. As is recognised by those authors who have written about Dee in any detail, he was a practising sorcerer and deeply involved in the occult, and Queen Elizabeth saw fit to use him as one of her more important and influential advisors. For convenience, and to save my readers from having to rely exclusively on my say-so in something that is of the utmost importance, I now quote directly from an article by Dr. Robert Poole entitled *John Dee and the English Calendar: Science, Religion and Empire*, 1996:

> One of the leading scientific figures in England, and possessed of one of the largest private libraries in the country, he had a command of the latest astronomical learning (Copernicus included) as well as of current antiquarian and historical writing.....
>
> Dee was also a long-time associate of the Elizabethan régime. He had been imprisoned under Queen Mary, had given astrological advice as to the date of Queen Elizabeth's coronation, had acted as agent for Walsingham, and with Walsingham was among the advocates of a "blue water" foreign policy combining Protestant alliances with voyages of exploration and colonisation.
>
> Dee has been credited with the popularisation, and one of the earliest uses, of the term "British Empire". This was well before the union of the crowns of England and Scotland gave the term "British" its modern use...
>
> In 1576-8 Dee had published a four-volume work under the general title of *The Brytish Monarchie*, in which he elaborated his imperial case. The well-known frontispiece to the volume on *The Art of Navigation* (1577) carried an image of the "Imperiall Ship" of Christendom, carrying the Empress Elizabeth on a mission to restore her empire through sea power. The same work carried extensive hydrographical tables,

entitled "The Brytish Queene Elizabeth, Her Tables Gubernautik", an idea prefiguring "Queen Elizabeth's perpetual calendar". Historical recovery, geographical expansion and mathematical advance went hand in hand. He followed this four-volume work by drawing up for the queen her "Titles to far lands", two manuscript rolls setting out her descent and title to the empires of Brutus and Arthur.

"Good gracious!" – I perhaps hear some of my readers saying to themselves. "Can it be that this little-known man was a key factor in the foundation of the biggest empire – indeed by far the biggest empire – that has ever existed? Can it be, too, that, but for him, the United States of America would not even be an English-speaking nation?"

Be that as it may, I ask my readers not to be deceived by the scientific *appearance* of the word "astrology" into thinking that it represents any form of genuine science. Page 57 of the *The Blackwell Dictionary of Western Philosophy* has this to say in its entry on astrology:

Astrology presupposes that a person's fate has been determined and written in the stars and leaves no place for human freedom. It has been a target of criticism in the Western rationalist tradition and is not presented as a prime example of a **pseudo-science.** (Bold-type in the original.)

Well, as we have just seen:

Dee was involved in what, under that grand-sounding terminology, was in fact black magic, termed "sorcery" in his day;

and he had a close relationship with Queen Elizabeth;

and she even went so far as to rely on him for her choice of the date for her coronation.

For further assistance on this topic I now re-introduce one of Francis Bacon's many biographers, Jean Overton Fuller, whom we met in chapter 4. In her book *Sir Francis Bacon – A Biography* (George Mann Books, Maidstone, Kent, revised edition, 1994), she informs her readers:

Dr. Dee chose for her a date and time astrologically apt for her coronation.

Did she say that this date was apt *astrologically*?

Reminding ourselves that astrology is the science – or, rather, what I maintain is very clearly in reality the *supposed* science – of foretelling future events by studying the positions of the planets and other celestial bodies in the sky, we should do well to wonder if Francis Bacon had an involvement with Dr. Dee in sorcery as well. The cunning and love of secrecy that we have seen to be a prominent feature of Bacon make it unwise to rule out this possibility.

This *possibility*, did I say? Merely a *possibility*?

Please, good readers, advert to the horrifying reality of occult involvement that emerged when we looked at the play *Macb*th*. Please advert, too, to the truly frightful catalogue of instance after instance after instance of violence of all kinds featuring in the plays of Shakespeare, which I needed to exercise considerable diligence to put together in chapter 8.

An *overwhelming likelihood*, even verging on *certainty*, would surely more appropriately indicate the extent of the possibility in question. The late Sir Lawrence Olivier, widely rated as the greatest Shakespearean actor in the history of the theatre, once famously said that with Shakespeare "we touch the face of God". Were *less* true words *ever* uttered? In all seriousness, I believe it could be argued that Olivier would have come closer to the truth if, in place of the words "...of God", he had said "...of the Devil".

*　　*　　*　　*　　*

Well, what, according to his messages that Mrs. Gallup succeeded in decoding, does Francis Bacon lead us to believe that he wrote, in addition to the Essays and the philosophical works that were published under his name? Using names sometimes borrowed and occasionally invented, his other writings included the following if we are to believe those ciphered messages. Restricting myself to just a sample of the writings of each supposed author:

The works of Edmund Spenser, including *Shepheard's Calendar* and *The Faerie Queene First Part* and *Second Part.*

...of Christopher Marlowe, such as *Tamburlane, Doctor Faustus* and *The Jew of Malta.*

...of Stephen Gosson, *Schoole of Abuse, containing a pleasant invective against Poets, Pipers, Plaiers, Jesters and suchlike Caterpillars of the Commonwealth* (1579). and few pamphlets. *Apologie for Poetrie*, and *Pleasant Quippes for Upstart New-fangled Gentlewomen.*

...of John Lyly, *Euphues' Anatomy of Wit.*

...of George Peele, *Edward I*; *The Arraignment of Paris.*

...of Robert Greene, *Orlando Furioso*; *Friar Bacon*; *James IV of Scotland.*

...of Thomas Kidd and sometimes Kyd, *The Spanish Tragedy.*

...of Thomas Nashe, *Summer's Last Will and Testament* and *Dido.*

...of William Webbe, *Discourse of English Poetrie.*

...of Thomas Watson, consisting of various translations from and into the classical languages.

...of Dr. Timothe Bright, *Treatise of Melancoly* (1586) and *Characterie* (1588).

...of Robert Burton, *Treatise of Melancholy* (1621)

...and of others as well.

What was to happen to Francis Bacon when his mother, Queen Elizabeth, died?

Those readers whose reaction is to dismiss as fantasy and absurdity the whole story represented, or they might say *supposedly* represented, by the material deciphered, or *supposedly* deciphered, by Mrs. Gallup, have solidly on their side the weight of academia, almost in its entirety. Such scholars as have addressed the subject in the context of her claims have held, almost universally, that there are no hidden messages, and that the letters A and B in the original published works are not even distinguishable in the way that she claims them to be.

Moreover, these experts could hardly "shout" their position more strongly than they do. Here, for instance, is a sample of what Sir Sidney Lee, the first biographer of William Shakespeare, and rated by many as the most authoritative of his biographers, says in the Appendix II, titled "The Bacon-Shakespeare controversy", of his *A Life of William Shakespeare* that was published in various editions between 1898 and 1915. (In what follows, the italicising of some of the colourful pieces of language that he uses in his efforts to crush the "anti-Shakespeareans" is mine.)

The apparent contrast between the homeliness of Shakespeare's Stratford career and the breadth of observation and knowledge displayed in his literary work has evoked the *fantastic* theory that Shakespeare was not the author of the literature that passes under his name. *Perverse attempts* have been made either to pronounce the authorship of his works an open question, or to assign them to his contemporary, Francis Bacon (1561-1626), the great prose-writer, philosopher and lawyer.

Equally ludicrous endeavours have been made to transfer Shakespeare's responsibility to the shoulders of our contemporaries beside Bacon....

Sir Edwin Durning-Lawrence *freakishly* credited Bacon with the composition, not only of Shakespeare's works, but almost all the great literature of his time....

All the argument bears witness to a phase of more or less *morbid process* of scepticism...

Since Sir Sidney now finds himself, in effect, sneering contemptuously, not only at contemporaries of his, but at me as well, and also at those of my readers who are not dismissing what is being argued in this chapter, I consider myself to be justified in offering a measured and forthright response.

For a start, I strongly recommend, to those with time to spare, Sir Sidney's book as a strong candidate for the title, the most remarkable book ever written.

I do not believe that that is an exaggeration.

In the first place, other than once on the very first page, where he gives the name of the first recorded holder of the family name as "Shakespeare or 'Shakspere' ", he uses the name "Shakespeare", thus spelt, not only for the Stratford man himself but also for every single member of the family, and even for their ancestors – and, of course, without *ever* giving the slightest indication

(a) that that name was *not* in fact the real name,

and

(b) that it had *never once been used* as a name by *anyone* up until that time.

This means that the entire book, and also almost every individual page of it, consists of falsification.

In the second place, the book consists of no fewer than *766* pages, in which, however, the actual *facts* relating to Shaksper that are included anywhere in it take up the space, not of half that number of pages, not of a quarter of that number of pages, *but... of... not... even... as... much.... as... a... single... page.* This of course could not be otherwise, given how few facts of any kind relating to Will Shaksper are on record.

Please, good reader, return to chapter 2 of this PART II of this book that you are reading now, to give yourself a quick reminder of the summary of all the known facts relating to William Shaksper that I gave there as fully as I reasonably could.

I think I can be justifiably confident that, once you have done that, you will agree with me that those words of mine a few paragraphs back, "a strong candidate for the title, the most remarkable book ever written", are almost an understatement. It is indeed something of a wonder that Lee even found it *possible* to do what he did. 766 pages! It perhaps says something to the discredit of the general reading public that it was a best-seller immediately on publication and ran to as many as *seven* editions.

As I take leave of Sir Sidney, I should make it clear that he is far from being on his own in his use of searingly scathing language when denouncing those who hold it to be impossible that Shaksper could be the same person as Shakespeare. Rather, he is far from untypical; and this of course is notwithstanding Mrs. Gallup's gracious and reasonable plea that her readers should weigh up and judge her book, as I also ask *this* book that you are now reading to be judged, "with the same intelligence and impartiality they would themselves desire if the presentation were their own."

*   *   *   *   *

There are of course massive vested interests pushing in the direction of clinging to the traditional position on the author of the works of Shakespeare.

For a start, there is the suffering of various kinds that the many supposed experts on Shakespeare would undergo in having to admit, *even if only to themselves* (but of course very much *not* only to themselves), that they had been wrong for so long.

Then there is the fact that they would be well aware:

(a) that the admission that they had been wrong, which of course would inescapably imply that all their colleagues who hold the traditional position are *also* wrong, would provoke strong, permanent and often public hostility towards them in at least the great majority of their fellow-members of their profession; and

(b) that such fellow-members would have strong motives to bring about the destruction of the reputations of those who dared to stick their necks out.

Perhaps most important of all, Shakespeare, as he is, *is an industry*, and a very large one, with even, for instance, as noted back in chapter 1 of PART I, *a whole town*, that of Stratford-upon-Avon in Warwickshire, depending on him for its present well-being and prosperity. Such industries would of course find it objectionable even only to be laughed at, let alone to have their very existence threatened.

*   *   *   *   *

The fact of academia having vested interests in the *status quo* does not prove those holding the traditional Shakespeare position to be wrong, of course. There is, however, much that does, in my submission.

An important reality is that, as mentioned earlier, the only alternative to Mrs. Gallup's account being what she claimed it to be is that she made the entire story up, and has been joined in doing that by others who have done further work on what is claimed to be the ciphered material.

Well, not only is she very evidently, as we have seen, simply not that kind of woman, but her book is not that kind of book, and no one examining it even cursorily could justify thinking for a moment that it was. It consists of nearly five hundred pages put together with painstaking labour, and copiously illustrated both with the original texts and with the letters in their many different shapes, and with everything that needs analysing being *thoroughly* analysed. Bluntly, those who claim that the author is insincere or misled have simply not paid sufficient attention to her heart-felt request to her readers to judge her book "with the same intelligence and impartiality they would themselves desire if the presentation were their own".

There is of course, an alternative to considering Mrs. Gallup to be a deceiver. This is the possibility that the story was made up by the original author of the material that she translated. Although this alternative needs more thorough examination than the first one, it too can be shown clearly to be completely unrealistic. There are many too many *external* facts that, once the story is known, can be seen to fit exactly into that story for it to be possible for such a story to be an invention.

*   *   *   *   *

Here I interrupt myself briefly to say that this is a point of the greatest importance in this context.

Once again, I ask for my readers' close attention as I elaborate a little on it.

It is very foreseeable that readers of Mrs. Gallup's book who are intrinsically hostile to what I claim to be her findings that are set out in it

(a) will dismiss those findings, or, in their view, "findings", and

(b) will make the allegation that I have put forward an exotic and, if common-sense is applied, hopelessly non-credible case; the case referred to being the case that is based on my acceptance of the imaginative writings of an American lady, Mrs. Elizabeth Wells Gallup, who came up with the story that I have been relating and claimed that she had unearthed it by deciphering certain writings of Francis Bacon.

Ladies and gentlemen, that would *not* correctly represent my position. What *would* correctly represent it is this.

Mrs. Gallup's offering to her readers is, on the face of it, sufficiently eye-opening to deserve careful consideration, under two headings, of which I have already made mention but are worth repeating and emphasising.

First heading: –

Mrs. Gallup gives every indication of being genuinely scholarly, which includes being conscientious and honest.

Second heading, and arguably even more important, if anything *could* be more important than what has just been outlined under the first heading: –

Everything that Mrs. Gallup relates to her readers fits in with the facts – the *verifiable* facts – as no piece of fiction possibly could; and... and... *and...*, what is more, these verifiable facts include some facts *that were not accessible to Mrs. Gallup when she was doing her research.*

For instance, whereas the portraits of Francis Bacon, Robert Dudley and Queen Elizabeth that have survived show a sufficient similarity of features in them to make it completely credible Bacon is the son of Dudley and the Queen, Sir Nicholas and Lady Bacon, providentially, are so *utterly* different in appearance from Bacon that the supposed parentage is virtually impossible.

I am not relying on my own opinion alone in saying that.

One of Francis Bacon's many biographers, Jean Overton Fuller, whom we have met in previous pages, was sufficiently sceptical about whether he could be the legitimate son of his official parents to take it upon herself to raise the matter with specialist experts on genetics. As she records in chapter 2 of her *Sir Francis Bacon – A Biography*, all those whom she consulted agreed that the possibility of legitimacy could nearly be ruled out completely, and the most eminent of them all, Professor Briscoe Ford, Fellow of the Royal Society and of All Souls, and Emeritus Professor of Genetics at Oxford, was prepared to be quoted as saying that the chances of Bacon's being the actual son of Sir Nicholas and Lady Bacon were less than one in one hundred thousand, less that a thousandth of 1%. (Interestingly, a portrait of the Earl of Essex shows, on exactly the same basis, that it is *also* possible for *Essex* to have been a son of Dudley and the Queen.)

It is, incidentally, telling that Mrs. Gallup did not make any mention of these likenesses and "unlikenesses" in her book. Had she been aware of them, she certainly would have, since – as we are now about to see – they give strong support for her case. Clearly, therefore, she was unaware of them; and her findings, in consequence, are *independent* of any such evidence that adds confirmation to them, and are, in further consequence, all the more powerful as confirmations of Mrs. Gallup's case.

On this and the next two pages are some relevant pictures, together with, in each case, the name of the person that the picture represents.

Scarcely less compelling than those pictures, as confirmation of what Mrs. Gallup has been telling us, is the following, which is fully on record. Although Francis Bacon's relations with his parents or supposed parents were never unharmonious, nevertheless, when Sir Nicholas, an extremely rich man, died in 1579, he made provision in his published and carefully drawn-up will for the distribution of his estate to all his seven children *other than Francis*, for whom the will made no provision of any kind.

Francis was *mentioned* in the will, but he received nothing. I suggest that *this fact even by itself* gives confirmation – confirmation, what is more, that is *completely clear-cut* – of Mrs. Gallup's revelation that Francis was only a *nominal* member of the family, which meant that he could be expected to be very adequately provided for elsewhere.

Robert Dudley, Earl of Leicester

Sir Francis Bacon, Viscount St. Albans

Sir Francis Bacon, Viscount St. Albans (another portrait)

Robert Devereux, Earl of Essex

Robert Dudley, Earl of Leicester

Queen Elizabeth I, "The Virgin Queen"

Sir Nicholas Bacon

Sir Nicholas Bacon

Lady (Anne) Bacon　　　Lady (Anne) Bacon

If that were to need any further support, which I suggest that it does not, it is to be found in the fact that Francis *was indeed* separately provided for. In the following year, he took up residence in the house and estate of Twickenham Park in south-west London.

It is not known how it came about that this became his home. Some think that a lease was given to him by Edward Bacon, one of his half-brothers, although there is no remotely adequate evidence of that. Others have thought that it was arranged by the Queen. Whatever the solution, what is definite is (a) that Sir Nicholas left him no inheritance for no *apparently* good reason, and (b) that his supposed son was able, shortly afterwards, to take possession of a substantial property, *also* for no apparently good reason.

More evidence: there is something mysterious about Francis Bacon's baptism. It took place in the St. Martin-in-the-Fields Church in Trafalgar Square, and the words of the registration of the baptism there in 1561 are:

25 Januarie Baptizatus fuit Mr. Franciscos Bacon.

What possible reason, other than for it to be on record that something very unusual was involved, could there have been for using the word "Mr." in the record of an infant's baptism, of which no other example in baptismal records is known? According to Virginia M. Fellows, a diligent researcher, after noting, on page 24 of her book *The Shakespeare Code* (1st Books Library, 2000), the title "Mr." was not generally used for baptism, makes the additional point that it was not used for the *other* sons of the Bacons, goes on to ask:

> Why was it added to Francis's name? Could it have been an unexpected date of respect for this particular child?
>
> Even more puzzling – there seems to have been an attempt by later hands to erase the title out of the registry, although the original writing can in fact still be seen.

Another mystery that finds a solution if the cipher is authentic is the relationship between Queen Elizabeth and the Earl of Essex. In many books in which Queen Elizabeth's life is treated in some detail, their relationship is extraordinary, with him having access to her sleeping quarters at will, with the effect that, even though he was more than thirty years younger, she was thought to have been his mistress – which would be at least *verging* on being weird, a factor which is strangely overlooked by historians who mention their relationship. His being her son of course transforms that rather perverse-appearing relationship into a completely normal one.

*   *   *   *   *

Could any further evidence be needed in support of the proposition that, in Francis Bacon, we have already found the real William Shakespeare? Actually *needed*, surely not; but there is one last fact, a widely known one, that is worth bringing into the picture, because, although it does not quite fall into the category of *evidence*, it can at least be considered comforting *confirmation* of what the foregoing evidence and reasoning have led us to.

This is the term "the Bard of Avon" that was first used by the actor David Garrick in 1769 as representing Shakespeare and has now become so common as to be virtually official.

The word "bard" in that adopted title means of course minstrel or travelling poet, but if you consult any dictionary that aims at reasonable completeness, such as, for instance, the *Concise Oxford Dictionary*, you will find included in the definitions of "bard" the term "a thin slice of bacon" – yes, "of *bacon*" – or similar. No other well-known poet is commonly referred to as a bard, let alone as "*The* Bard" of somewhere-or-other. It is surely reasonable to wonder if the title "the Bard of Avon" is either an insider's joke or even a clue, deliberately planted by someone "in the know". Although not in the realm of certainty, it seems at least as likely that that is the case as that the overlapping of the term with the *real* author's name is pure coincidence.

Queen Elizabeth was William Shakespeare's *mother*? Yes, I did suggest, back in the Preface, that of all the topics that have been subjects for discussion since the dawn of recorded history, I doubted if there had ever been a more *interesting* one than the one addressed in this book; and the discovery Elizabeth and Shakespeare had as close a family-relationship as can exist would, I submit, be even on its own just about enough to justify that claim.

*   *   *   *   *

It has now emerged as a possibility that is perhaps strong enough to be suitably described even as a very great *probability* that "William Shakespeare" was the son, and, what is more, the *legitimate* son, of one of the most revered of all England's mon-archs. Yes, it really does seem to be the case that the Bard of Avon was legitimately entitled to address the Virgin Queen as "Mummy"! – and, for that matter, King Henry VIII as "Grandpa", if their lives had overlapped, which they did not. (King Henry died in 1547; Francis Bacon was born in 1560.)

In our quest to find out as much about Shakespeare as we can that is of any significant importance, which must include, out of fairness, a strict obligation to find out all that we can that is in his favour, it is appropriate to have a reasonably close look at this lady who now appears to have been his mother. We need not

134

concern ourselves with King Henry VIII, since both the breeding and the chronology are too distant.

Chapter 7
And if it be the case that…?

On the face of it, we have *at last* come across something that William Shakespeare and Francis Bacon and their up-till-now enthusiastic admirers can be pleased with and even proud of.

Queen Elizabeth I, it seems, did much to earn the applause of her subjects, and indeed of all future generations up to the present day. Often referred to affectionately as "Good Queen Bess", she is generally considered to come closer than any other English monarch to King Canute the Great and King Alfred the Great in deserving to be known as "the Great". Indeed, a book about her published in 1958, by the well-regarded historian the late Elizabeth Jenkins, is actually called *Elizabeth the Great.*

The generality of historians share Elizabeth Jenkins's view of her, and indeed do so wholeheartedly, even extravagantly. Here, from three fairly-recently published books, is a representative sample, of what they say about her.

The English and Their History by Robert Tombs (Penguin Books, 2015, page 179):

> Her virtues, and vices, did much to keep the country safe throughout her long reign. However one describes them, these characteristics – caution, cunning, cleverness, procrastination – give her some claim to be considered England's greatest monarch.'

A Short History of England by Simon Jenkins (Profile Books, 2011, page 131):

> She had brought her nation glory and peace. Elizabeth was surely the greatest of England's rulers.

Elizabeth the Queen by Alison Weir (Vintage, 2009), in its preface:

> Queen Elizabeth was such a fascinating and charismatic character that her life as a queen merits a book on its own…
>
> This is a study of personal government at its best… She identified herself with her people and worked for their common

interests. She brought peace and stability to her troubled kingdom. She nurtured it as a mother nurtures a child...

The Queen... also brought unity to her people by effecting a religious compromise that has lasted until this day, and by making herself an enduring focus of their loyalty. She had enjoyed a unique relationship with her subjects which had never been before and has never been since. Few Queens have been so loved...

The most fitting epitaph to this extraordinary woman is to be found in Camden's biography. "No oblivion shall ever bury the glory of her name; for her happy and renowned memory still liveth and shall forever in the minds of men... A strong, well-educated ruler loved by her courtiers and people alike."

Included in this summary of the general picture of Queen Elizabeth that I am giving at this point must be the name "Gloriana", which first appeared, during her reign, in Edmund Spenser's *Faerie Queen* where it clearly had reference to her. She swiftly assumed this name for herself, and under it she is more honoured even by *today's* Royal Family than are any of today's Royal Family's other predecessors. "Gloriana" is the name of the royal barge, with its gilded prow, that is now used by the Royal Family on the Thames, and was, for instance, part of the celebration of Her present Majesty's Diamond Jubilee when, transporting the Royal Family, it led a flotilla of some fifty boats under Tower Bridge, where the Tower canon boomed the traditional sixty-two-gun salute.

Queen Elizabeth I was a true successor to King Alfred the Great, it seems. Can we *at last* engage ourselves in rejoicing, on behalf of our real William Shakespeare, Francis Bacon?

*   *   *   *   *

Sad to say, it does not seem possible to agree that those representations of Queen Elizabeth – which are similar to those put forward by most historians – have even the remotest approach to reality. Rather, a not-inappropriate question could even be, and I am choosing my words carefully: could Queen Elizabeth justly be described as the single most evil woman in the whole of recorded history?

Drastically opposed to the general picture of her given by virtually all the most respected historians though the implications of that question are, please be assured that I do not put it lightly. I shall now give what I believe to be sufficient reasons to justify it, while inviting my readers to keep in their minds, as they read what follows, another question: can they think of any historical figure who could be credibly considered to be her superior, or at least her equal, in entitlement to that terrible label?

*   *   *   *   *

Before I go any further, however, I think it appropriate to give a few words of background to my use of the sources that I shall be quoting from.

Many decades ago, I found myself with the need to do extensive research into the history of England, and not least of her Kings and Queens. Please make no mistake. The need for such research faces *everyone* who wishes to arrive at truth in relation to English history. Again and again, there are situations in history when people have motives to falsify it and are well placed to do the falsifying.

Lest there be any of my readers who doubt this important fact, I now offer three succinct statements on the subject by prominent figures of the past who were clearly in a good position to know what they were talking about.

My first witness: the founding father of the mass-produced motorcar, Mr. Henry Ford, in 1921:

History is bunk.

My second quotation, usually attributed to Sir Winston Churchill, explains why this is to be expected:

History is written by the victors.

In consequence of that fact, according to a third expert on the subject, the Emperor Napoleon Bonaparte, writing during the period when he was confined as a prisoner on the island of St. Helena in the closing years of his life:

History is nothing but the lies that are no longer disputed.

What follows from what those three knowledgeable authorities have just told us is, clearly, that history is an *exceptionally* interesting subject.

What is more, nowhere, I think I can safely say, is history *more* interesting than in the really *astounding* contrast between, on the one hand, the picture of Queen Elizabeth that is usually given by historians – and as has just given by the authors Robert Tombs, Simon Jenkins and Alison Weir whom I quoted above – and, on the other hand, the *reality* of that queen.

That being the case – and I think I shall be showing it very definitely to be the case – it is as appropriate here as anywhere for me to do what I have often been doing in these pages: to make direct use of writers who can be recognised as reliable at least on the particular subject for which I am using their help.

In this case it is easy to see why we can be justified in supposing their reliability. In the first place, they all make it evident that they did whatever research was needed to come up with the relevant information that we shall be looking at. In the second place, they were all of the same religious persuasion as that of Queen Elizabeth and therefore had no motive based on any religious prejudice to be in opposition to her.

My first witness is an uncompromisingly anti-Catholic legal historian, W. F. Finlason, writing in his own name in an edition of the important legal treatise, Reeves's *History of English Law*, that was edited by him and originally published in 1869. In what now follows the italicisations are mine.

The law and legislation of the present reign [Queen Elizabeth's] upon the subject of religion were based upon the principle of despotism, and in that respect were marked by the same spirit as that which had pervaded the reign of Henry VIII and Edward VI. In a word it was the spirit of tyranny.

The rapacity which characterised the previous reigns was equally characteristic of the present. *The conduct of Elizabeth with regard to the Church was worse than that of the worst tyrants of the Norman sovereigns.* During the whole of her reign the confiscatory laws passed under Henry VIII and Edward VI were rigidly enforced, *and all colleges, or hospitals, or charities which had escaped their rapacity were seized by the queen. The system of confiscation involved many charities that were not obnoxious to the law* – that is to say, were doing no harm.

At her coronation, Queen Elizabeth took the ancient and customary oath – the same oath that Queen Mary had taken a few years earlier – to maintain 'the laws and customs granted to [the people of England] by the ancient kings of England, and especially the laws, customs and privileges granted to the clergy and people by the glorious King St. Edward [the Confessor] (1042–66 . . . and towards God, Holy Church, and to clergy and people, peace and accord in God..."

As we shall be seeing, she kept that solemn oath *for just six weeks.*

For my second of the three sources that I am using in my project to show Queen Elizabeth I as she really was, I have chosen a book on English history that can fairly be rated as remarkable to an extent that can fairly be described as spectacular.

To show its value for our purpose, it needs some introduction.

The real facts relating to both the reign and the character of Queen Elizabeth, are in such contradiction to what is commonly supposed by historians, and therefore by most other people as well, that it is especially useful and valuable in that, in the source that I am now about to make use of, there is no element of prejudice against the Protestant religion that might be expected to lead to those facts being distorted, even slightly. I have indeed been fortunate in being able to make use of a book written by an author whose religious persuasion would incline him, if any direction, to be in fundamental *opposition* to what he found himself having to say about Queen Elizabeth.

Because of the controversial nature of what follows, and in particular because of what we have just read, courtesy of the historians Elizabeth Jenkins, Robert Tombs and Alison Weir, it is as well, before we start using this author and his book, to show why its author can safely be relied upon as completely trustworthy. This will take up some space; but I believe it to be necessary because what is coming is so intrinsically contentious that it is even more than usually important that readers can put complete trust in what is being said.

The book in question is *A History of the Protestant Reformation in England and Ireland,* originally put together under the sole authorship of William Cobbett back in the early nineteenth century.

Cobbett was born in 1763, in Farnham in Surrey, to parents in the lower ranks of society. After an education extending to little more than being taught to read and write by his father, at age of seventeen he impulsively decided to migrate to London. After working there for a few months as a lawyer's clerk, he enlisted in the army and, mostly in America, spent eight years in the ranks, never becoming an officer. To his lasting benefit, he used the considerable amount of spare time available to non-officers to make a careful and thorough study of the English language, and in particular of English grammar, which he mastered to the extent of being able to teach it to occasional non-English-speakers in America that he came across.

While still in the army, he took up writing about controversial political subjects, and at once his output was impressive enough for some of it to be reprinted in England and to make him well known there.

In 1800, he resigned from the army and returned to England. There he found himself, because of what he had written, a prominent public figure – so much so, indeed, as to be invited by the then-Prime Minister, William Pitt, to be editor of the official government newspaper.

He decided that he did not want to be a direct agent of the Government, however, and turned the offer down. Instead, in 1801, he started up his own weekly newspaper, *The Political Register*, which developed a huge circulation nationwide, was right from the start remarkably influential, and continued in existence until his death thirty-four years later.

In 1803, war broke out between England and France, of which, soon afterwards, Napoleon Bonaparte was to become its first Emperor. Cobbett's response to this new development was to write and publish a pamphlet called *Important Considerations for the People of the Kingdom*, which he put together principally to warn the nation of the consequences that could be expected to follow from a French invasion.

So compellingly written was this pamphlet that Henry Addington, who by then had replaced William Pitt as England's Prime Minister, responded to it by arranging for copies to be sent to every parish in the kingdom. Its consequent effect on the entire English public was immediate and considerable.

For a little while longer, Cobbett's popularity with leading Members of both Houses of Parliament continued to grow. For instance, the Duke of Kent of the day hailed him as "this great British patriot" and the Government's Secretary at War, William Windham, extravagantly went as far as to say that he deserved "a statue of gold" for the services that he had rendered to Britain while in America.

This popularity did not last, however, at least in Government circles. As early as in 1801 he had started publicly questioning some of the Government's policies. By 1804, by which time William Pitt – "Pitt the Younger", the son of the William Pitt who, as Prime Minister had invited him to edit the Government newspaper – had, extraordinarily, become, at the age of twenty-four, the youngest Prime Minister there had ever been and indeed is ever likely to be, Cobbett was wholeheartedly attacking some of them.

Eventually, those in Government whom Cobbett was opposing, and too effectively for their liking, struck back; and, when he went so far as to denounce, in his *Political Register*, the officially prescribed flogging of some non-professional soldiers, he ended up, in 1810, being prosecuted for what was termed "treasonous libel", found guilty, and sentenced to two years imprisonment in Newgate prison.

Not that this affected his general popularity in England: after his release, a formal dinner with no fewer than six hundred guests was held in his honour.

By 1816, the Government was finding *The Political Register* so offensive that Cobbett had to leave the country for his safety. He returned to the United States, where one of his most notable accomplishments was the composition of a book called *Grammar of the English Language* that was an immediate best-seller, a remarkable achievement by someone who had had only minimal formal education. Even now, published by the Oxford University Press, it is still in print. His father, who, as we have seen, was his original teacher of how to write English, deserves our applause!

In 1819 Cobbett was able to return to England safely, where he continued his literary output. Four of his books of this period were especially liked and admired by his reading public:

  – His *Cottage Economy*, written to teach cottagers self-sufficiency skills such as bread-making and beer-brewing;

  – *Rural Rides*, which he is best known for and which has never been out of print. It is an account of a series of journeys on horseback by him through parts of the English countryside for the purpose of reporting and commenting on what he saw from the viewpoint of both the farmer that he then was and the social reformer that he also was.

  – *Advice to Young Men*. This was an attack on a book, *An Essay on the Principle of Population*, whose author, the Rev. Thomas Robert Malthus, maintained in it that, while, at present birth-rates, the population could be expected to increase "at a geometrical ratio", doubling every twenty-five years, during the same period of time the production of food could only increase at the very much lower "arithmetical ratio", a difference that would lead to famine unless steps were taken to decrease birth rates.

   – *A History of the Protestant Reformation in England and Ireland*, the book that I shall shortly be making use of.

Four times, in 1806, 1820, 1826 and 1832, Cobbett tried to become a Member of Parliament. Three times he was unsuccessful but on the fourth attempt he was elected, whereupon he at once set about attacking corruption in government, in doing so making himself far from popular with his fellow-M.P.s.

Three years later he died, a few miles from the town Farnham, in Surrey, in which he had been born.

Thus some background to the book of which I am about to make use. It remains to show why it can be trusted as can few other books, if any, that deal with that period.

Chapter 8

Justifying making use of William Cobbett in this context.

What Cobbett's *History of the Protestant Reformation* was essentially about was a long-running war. This conflict was between:

On the one hand, the Protestant religion that had started to come into being in the early 16th century, when King Henry VIII broke with Rome and made himself head of the Church of England, and after which it was further developed in the reigns of King Edward VI and Queen Elizabeth I.

On the other hand, the Catholic religion to which England had been converted by the Benedictine monk Augustine, who succeeded in converting England to Christianity at the end of the sixth century A.D.; became the first Archbishop of Canterbury in 1597; and later was canonised as Saint Augustine of Canterbury.

I rate Cobbett's *History of the Protestant Reformation*, I believe fairly, as one of the most remarkable books on any period of history that have ever been written, and what will be following shortly on the subject of Queen Elizabeth I is taken from it.

Giving, I think, justification of what I have just claimed on behalf of the book are the combined facts, remarkable to an extent that I believe can fairly be described as spectacular, that,

on the one hand Cobbett was a Protestant – a member of the Church of England – in his beliefs and practices,

while, on the other hand, he had sufficient intellectual honesty to consider himself morally bound to defend the Catholic Church when he saw it attacked in a manner that was clearly unjust.

The reason that I have thought it appropriate, even verging on necessary, to make use of his book here is:

(a) that what is covered in the next chapter is at least as controversial as anything else dealt with in these pages, and

(b) that there are exceptionally good reasons to accept Cobbett's book as sound on the information given in it and in the opinions that he expresses in it.

Of these "exceptionally good reasons", here are the two principal ones.

The first is – as Cobbett makes clear, even emphasises, in the book – the solidity of his Protestant religious position (which indeed he retained for the rest of his life). From this it of course followed that, far from being influenced by any in-built prejudice in favour of the Catholic religion, he had no personal motive to defend that religion.

The second is that, some seventy years after Cobbett's original publication of the book, in instalments, during the years 1824-1827, it was re-introduced to the public by a notable Catholic scholar, the Rev. Francis Aidan Gasquet, later to become Cardinal Francis Aidan Gasquet. Having recognised its value as a defence against the anti-Catholic propaganda that was very much a feature of that time, Gasquet took considerable trouble with the new edition, improving its presentation and extensively adding footnotes on disputable points. Of interest for our purpose is something that he says in the Preface that he added at the beginning of the book.

> For the purpose of this edition, I have been at some pains to enquire into the truth of the assertions made, and to set down the results in the shape of notes, either giving authorities which may be taken to bear out the writer's statements, or pointing out wherein, in my opinion, Cobbett is mistaken, or has somewhat mis-stated or exaggerated the bearing of some fact. I confess that I was surprised to find how few were the instances in which some unsatisfactory authority could not be found to bear out the picture presented in the book's pages.

In short, we do not only have, in this book, a piece of literature and a source of information brought into existence with *very* diligent care for accuracy on the part of Cobbett, an experienced writer, that was obviously of the highest necessity in a controversial book that could be expected to have a wide readership because of who he was. We *also* have the benefit of, seven decades later, a thorough checking of the book by a highly competent scholar who had every motive to make sure that it contained, whether in the facts included in it or even in the opinions expressed in it, no inaccuracies of any kind.

Let us now see what, after that lengthy background to Cobbett and his book that I thought it as well to give, we can learn from Cobbett about Shakespeare's Mum.

Chapter 9
William Shakespeare's mother: the horrifying *reality*?

What follows is mainly a summary of the relevant information provided by Cobbett in the numbered paragraphs 260 onwards of his *A History of the Protestant Reformation in England and Ireland*, sometimes supplemented, as at the beginning, by direct quotations from that book.

> During the reign of her brother King Edward VI, Elizabeth had been a Protestant, and during the reign of her sister Queen Mary, she had been a Catholic. At the time of her sister Queen Mary's death, she not only went to mass publicly, but had a Catholic chapel in her house and also a confessor.
>
> These appearances had not, however, deceived her sister who, to the very last, doubted her sincerity. On her death-bed, honest and sincere Queen Mary required from her a frank avowal of her opinions as to religion. Elizabeth, in answer, prayed God that the earth might open and swallow her if she were not a true Roman Catholic...

Keep that last sentence in your minds, good readers, as we continue with Cobbett.

> It was, however, not long before the new Queen Elizabeth began the persecution of her unhappy subjects because they were Roman Catholics.
>
> She was illegitimate by law. The marriage of her mother Anne Boleyn had been, in accordance by an English law which yet remained unrepealed, declared to be null and void from the beginning. Her accession having, as was usual, been notified to overseas nations – that is to say, their having been told that "she had succeeded to the throne by hereditary right and the consent of the nation," the Pope answered that he could not understand the hereditary right of a person who had not been born in lawful wedlock, and that therefore he was unable to acknowledge her hereditary right.
>
> This of course was a strong inducement, for a lady whose conscience was as flexible as Elizabeth's, to resolve to be a Protestant.

There was also another motive, an even stronger one.

Mary Queen of Scotland claimed the throne as the nearest legitimate descendant of King Henry VII, so that Elizabeth ran a clear risk of losing the crown unless she first became a Protestant and then rammed Protestant beliefs down the throats of her people.

In short, she saw clearly that, if her people remained Roman Catholics, she could never reign in perfect safety. She knew that she had no hereditary right, because the law ascribed her birth to adultery on the part of King Henry VIII. She never could think of reigning quietly over people the Head of whose Church, the Pope, refused to acknowledge her rights to the Crown. Determined to wear that crown, she therefore resolved, cost whatever blood-shed it might, *to compel her people to abandon their religion* – the very religion that she had, a few months before, declared her belief in by praying to "God that the might open and swallow her alive if she were not a true Roman Catholic."

When Queen Mary died, Elizabeth's intention to change the religion of the country became, in a short time, so manifest that all bishops but one refused to crown her. She did at length find one who would do it, but even he would not agree to unless she conformed to the Catholic ritual.

As Cobbett then tells us, in 1559, in the first year of her reign, Queen Elizabeth enacted the Act of Uniformity.

Attacking at the very root the consciences of all Catholics in her realm, who constituted more than half the English population in 1559, this Act directed that the Catholic Mass, which had been the central part of the religion of England for more than a thousand years, should at once be outlawed.

From then on, the only church services that could legally be attended anywhere in England were the entirely *new* church services based on the new government-decreed, Protestant Book of Common Prayer.

Moreover, Sunday attendance of these services was *obligatory*, with huge fines for those who refused and *the penalty of death* for those who persevered in their refusal.

Stare at that, good readers, and struggle, if you need to, to believe it.

It gets worse.

All her subjects were obliged, *again on pain of death*, to take the oath of supremacy, thereby acknowledging the Queen's supremacy in "spiritual" matters and, in doing so, renouncing the Pope and becoming an apostate from the Catholic religion. In Cobbett's words:

> Thus was a very large part of her people at once condemned to death for adhering to the religion of their fathers, *and moreover for adhering to that very religion in which she had openly lived until she became queen, and, to her firm belief in which, she had sworn at her coronation.*

Further, it was made high treason for a priest to say Mass, or to come into the kingdom from abroad, and also for anyone to harbour a priest who said Mass.

Cobbett continues:

> Under such laws, hundreds upon hundreds were butchered in the most inhuman manner, being first hung up, then cut down *alive*, then their bowels ripped out and their bodies chopped into quarters – *only* because the unfortunate persons were too virtuous and sincere to apostatise from that Faith which *this queen herself* had at her coronation, in her coronation oath, solemnly sworn to adhere to and to defend!

Cobbett then asks:

> Where are you to find persecution and cruelty like this inflicted by Catholic princes?

> Elizabeth put, in one way or another, more Catholics to death *in one year*, for not becoming apostates to the religion *which she had sworn (a) to be her religion, and (b) to be the only true religion,* than Queen Mary put to death *in her whole reign*

for having apostatised from the religion of her and her fathers, and to which religion she had always adhered.

Yet the former is called, or has been called, "Good Queen Bess", and the latter "Bloody Queen Mary".

Is not what Cobbett has just told us truly fantastic?

And no, what Cobbett has just told us is not open to any sort of reasonable doubt. I offer for confirmation the greatly respected *Protestant* constitutional historian Henry Hallam, in his *Constitutional History of England*:

The Statute of Uniformity trenched [encroached] further on the natural rights of conscience.

It prohibited the use by a minister, whether beneficial or not, of any but the established liturgy.

For the first offence, the penalty was forfeiture of goods and chattels.

For the second offence, the penalty was a year's imprisonment.

For the first offence, the penalty was imprisonment for life,

Furthermore, it imposed a fine of one shilling *on all who would absent themselves from church on Sundays and holy days* [of which there were seventy-seven].

Since a skilled craftsman, such as a carpenter, could expect to earn about ten-pence (less than a shilling) a day, even a fine of a shilling would have been crippling for a large family.

Yet that was only the beginning. Later in Elizabeth's reign the head of a *non-conforming* family was subjected to a progressively accumulating monthly fine of £20 for the first month, £40 for the second, £60 for the third, up to a maximum of £200, when the *recusant* was bound over in the sum of £200 until he or she conformed – vast sums of money in those days.

* * * * *

No fewer than seven Acts of Parliament creating *new* treasonable offences were passed in Queen Elizabeth's reign. It will probably be sufficient for our purposes to look at a sickening but representative selection of just five of these, which we shall therefore now have the displeasure of doing.

A piece of important background to what is to follow is that the first Act of the first Parliament of so-called "Bloody Mary's" reign actually *reduced* the number of offences constituting treason, so that the only such offences that remained were those contained in King Edward III's Statute of Treasons of 1352. These addressed genuine treason and were necessary for the safety of the realm and its ordinary citizens.

Those of my readers who up until now have been embracing the concept of "Good Queen Bess" will surely have supposed that this new Queen – "so loved" by her people, according to Alison Weir in her book that I quoted from a few pages back – quickly set about outdoing Mary in liberalising the laws. Having recently looked at one of the first acts of Mary's reign, let us now look at the very first of the Acts of Elizabeth's reign, which I shall be numbering for convenience: "1 Elizabeth c.1", passed in 1558.

Number 1. Under this Act, (a) words spoken and written and (b) actions done against the Royal Supremacy – Supremacy that was now *spiritual* as well as temporal, let it be noted, since Queen Elizabeth was now grasping back what Queen Mary had voluntarily abandoned – were punishable as follows:

For a first offence, all real and personal property was forfeited, real property being immovable property such as land and buildings.

For a second offence, the penalties of *Praemunire* were inflicted. These penalties were loss of all civil rights, forfeiture of goods and chattels (movable property) as well as of land, and also imprisonment "during the royal pleasure".

For a third offence, *the penalties for high treason were inflicted*.

Numbers 2 and 3. So much for the First Act of Queen Elizabeth's reign. Two more acts followed, "5 Elizabeth c.1" and "13 Elizabeth c.1". Both of them drastically increased the scope of treason and changed its definition. Then, in 1581, a further act made it *high treason* to "reconcile or to be reconciled" to "the Romish Religion" ("23 Elizabeth c.2") – that is to say, the religion to which St. Augustine had converted the English only a thousand years before, and which had prevailed until the time of King Henry VIII, *and... which Queen Elizabeth had sworn, in a solemn oath at her coronation, to uphold.*

Number 4. Perhaps most remarkably of all, in 1585 an act ("27 Elizabeth c.2") was passed which made it high treason *merely to have been ordained a priest* in the religion which Elizabeth *had sworn by solemn oath to uphold.* This applied to anyone ordained from the time of the first year of her reign. Under this single statute alone, one hundred and twenty-three priests were hanged, drawn and quartered during the reign of Queen Elizabeth.

The fortunate people who harboured or gave comfort to priests were not in fact adjudged guilty of treason, but only of an *ordinary* felony. This meant that they were subjected *only* to hanging, rather than to hanging, drawing, cutting off the privy parts, and all the rest.

Number 5. Nor did Queen Elizabeth's efforts to be – in the words just quoted of Alison Weir – "so loved" by her people stop there. In "35 Elizabeth c.2" the following was enacted:

Anyone who during a month refused to attend public worship was committed to prison.

If those so committed to prison should persist in their refusal for three months, they were obliged to leave the country.

Those who refused to act in accordance with this condition or returned after being banished were subject to capital punishment as felons.

This last act, incidentally, was called "An Act to Retain Her Majesty's Subjects Within Due Obedience". *To retain their due obedience!* And what *kind* of obedience? *Religious* obedience was the obligation of the "loving" subjects of "Good Queen Bess", under penalty of imprisonment and then execution if their consciences forbade them to abandon the religion that Queen Elizabeth had solemnly sworn to uphold.

*　　*　　*　　*　　*

Queen Elizabeth's death was not a happy one. During her last illness she recalled a prophecy that she would die naturally in bed, and she therefore refused to go to bed, instead stretching herself out on cushions outside her bedroom.

There she remained for ten days, fully dressed, fasting and sleepless, with her eyes fixed on the ground and a finger always in her mouth, and uttering no word of repentance. When she was clearly close to death, the Archbishop of Canterbury and other prelates approached her, but she told them to get packing, declaring that she knew full well that they were "hedgepriests" – a colossal irony given that *she herself* had been responsible for the creation of these "ministers of God" whom she now denounced as worthless.

So much for Queen Elizabeth I, so greatly revered by most historians. By contrast with their opinion of her, in the previous chapter I put myself on record as wondering whether she could possibly have been the most evil woman that ever lived. I now put *this* question:

"What more would she have needed to do in order to earn that title?"

*　　*　　*　　*　　*

Thus the woman whom, as noted in the previous chapter, "William Shakespeare" credibly appears to have had the legitimate right to address as "Mother" – in this case a worthy mother, if I may permit myself just one unseemly sarcasm, of such a man.

She is surely of the utmost relevance to any assessment of Shakespeare that we may care to make, whether (a) because of the blood – indeed royal blood, we have now learnt – that flowed through his veins or (b) because of whatever influence she may have had on him after she took the decision that he should be made aware of their relationship.

Chapter 10
Shakespeare on the subject of Queen Elizabeth I.

Now that we know what we know about Queen Elizabeth I, which of course includes what we now know about her blood-relationship with Francis Bacon, it is worth, as a final offering under this heading, having a look at what he, Queen Elizabeth's elder son, had to say about his mother.

After her death, he had plenty of time to write a play about or a biography of her if he had wanted to, since she died in 1603 and he of course lived for many years after that, and even his most important mask, "William Shakespeare", the William Shaksper of Stratford-upon-Avon, did not die until 1605.

For some reason he did not take that step, but he did give, to the reading and theatre-going public of his day and thereafter, a written assessment of her. I wonder if those readers who have not yet been exposed to it would like to deduce or guess, from all that we have learnt about Bacon and his mother up to this point, what picture of her he decided to offer, conscious, of course, that, because of the power of his writing, what he came up with was likely to be in high degree influential.

What he wrote was certainly of interest.

On one hand, it can be considered commendable, in that, praising Queen Elizabeth "to the skies", as we shall be seeing, it fully conforms to the Fourth Commandment recorded in both Exodus 20:12 and Deuteronomy 5:16 of the Bible's Old Testament:

Honour thy father and thy mother.

On the other hand, however, it is about as directly and strongly opposed to reality – to what is actually *true* – as can be imagined.

What is under consideration in this context is the very last scene in the Shakespeare play *The Life of King Henry the Eighth*. What Mummy's boy, as it has emerged that Shakespeare is, has to say about Mummy – controversial figure, in the highest degree, as it has emerged that Queen Elizabeth I is – can surely be fairly described as important even to the possible extent of being uniquely important. It has seemed desirable, therefore, to say the least, to quote at least some of what Mummy's boy says about Mummy, in the only instance in which he went on record on this subject. I have therefore examined this scene with some care in an attempt to make a satisfactory assessment of which part or parts of the scene would be most suitable for this purpose.

In fact I ended up finding myself unable to find anything anywhere in Scene 4 of Act V of *The Life of King Henry the Eighth* that I would feel comfortable about not including. Here, therefore, against the background of a determination on my part not to risk short-changing my readers, is that scene in full, including even the stage directions at the beginning.

Before I start quoting, I ask of my readers two favours.

The first of them is to re-read the previous chapter, chapter 9, in order to remind yourself of the *reality* of Queen Elizabeth, before embarking on what now follows.

The second is to do the same re-reading once again *immediately after* reaching the end of this Scene 5.

In making this rather burdensome request, I am in fact paying Francis Bacon a handsome compliment: namely that his writing, in its power and in its ability to leave lasting impressions even in the context of exposing him as the pernicious intellectual swindler that he is, is so great that there are almost no precautions that would be too great to take in to prevent him from succeeding, even centuries after his death, in promoting his countless lies.

Please, good reader, get ready to shudder in horror when, after a short introduction, we arrive at Archbishop Cranmer's long speech.

SCENE 5. The palace.

Enter trumpets, sounding; then two Aldermen, Lord Mayor, Garter, CRANMER, NORFOLK with his marshal's staff, SUFFOLK, two Noblemen bearing great standing-bowls for the christening-

gifts; then four Noblemen bearing a canopy, under which the Duchess of Norfolk, godmother, bearing the child richly habited in a mantle, & a train borne by a Lady; then follows the March-ioness Dorset, the other godmother, and Ladies. The troop pass once about the stage, and Garter speaks.

Garter

Heaven, from thy endless goodness, send prosperous
life, long, and ever happy, to the high and mighty
princess of England, Elizabeth!

Flourish. Enter KING HENRY VIII and Guard

CRANMER [Kneeling]

And to your royal grace, and the good queen,
My noble partners, and myself, thus pray:
All comfort, joy, in this most gracious lady,
Heaven ever laid up to make parents happy,
May hourly fall upon ye!

KING HENRY VIII

Thank you, good lord archbishop: What is her name?

CRANMER

Elizabeth.

KING HENRY VIII

Stand up, lord.

KING HENRY VIII kisses the child and then addresses her:

With this kiss take my blessing: God protect thee!
Into whose hand I give thy life.

CRANMER

Amen.

KING HENRY VIII

My noble gossips, ye have been too prodigal:
I thank ye heartily; so shall this lady,
When she has so much English.

Please prepare yourselves, gracious readers. What Cranmer has been saying – deplorable as it is in the context of the manner in which the future Queen would be reigning over her subjects – is now about to become even worse.

Now continuing:

CRANMER

Let me speak, sir,
For heaven now bids me; and the words I utter
Let none think flattery, for they'll find 'em truth.
This royal infant – heaven still move about her! –
Though in her cradle, yet now promises
Upon this land a thousand thousand blessings,
Which time shall bring to ripeness: she shall be –
But few now living can behold that goodness –
A pattern to all princes living with her,
And all that shall succeed: Saba was never
More covetous of wisdom and fair virtue
Than this pure soul shall be: all princely graces,
That mould up such a mighty piece as this is,
With all the virtues that attend the good,
Shall still be doubled on her: truth shall nurse her,
Holy and heavenly thoughts still counsel her:
She shall be loved and fear'd: her own shall bless her;
Her foes shake like a field of beaten corn,
And hang their heads with sorrow: good grows with her:
In her days every man shall eat in safety,
Under his own vine, what he plants; and sing
The merry songs of peace to all his neighbours:
God shall be truly known; and those about her
From her shall read the perfect ways of honour,
And by those claim their greatness, not by blood.
Nor shall this peace sleep with her: but as when
The bird of wonder dies, the maiden phoenix,
Her ashes new create another heir,
As great in admiration as herself;
So shall she leave her blessedness to one,
When heaven shall call her from this cloud of darkness,
Who from the sacred ashes of her honour
Shall star-like rise, as great in fame as she was,
And so stand fix'd: peace, plenty, love, truth, terror,
That were the servants to this chosen infant,
Shall then be his, and like a vine grow to him:

Wherever the bright sun of heaven shall shine,
His honour and the greatness of his name
Shall be, and make new nations: he shall flourish,
And, like a mountain cedar, reach his branches
To all the plains about him: our children's children
Shall see this, and bless heaven.

KING HENRY VIII

Thou speakest wonders.

CRANMER

She shall be, to the happiness of England,
An aged princess; many days shall see her,
And yet no day without a deed to crown it.
Would I had known no more! but she must die,
She must, the saints must have her; yet a virgin,
A most unspotted lily shall she pass
To the ground, and all the world shall mourn her.

Chapter 11
Beginning the rounding-off of the authorship case.

What, then, are the practical consequences of accepting as certain, as I imagine open-minded readers may by now be thinking that we must do, that, out of the many writers contemporary to William Shakespeare who are claimed to be William Shakespeare, it was Francis Bacon who was really the author of the plays and sonnets attributed to William Shakespeare?

Without exception, all the authorship problems that facing us if it be insisted that Stratford's Will Shaksper is the author, vanish at once. Please consider the following.

– Perhaps most obviously of all, Francis Bacon, the greatest lawyer of his day, and even, as we have seen, honoured to this very day by a statue of him in Gray's Inn, would have had an effortless mastery of the legal terminology constantly used in the plays that has been admired and never found fault with by learned lawyers, including judges.

– Born and brought up by courtiers as he was, and having been part of court life from his earliest days, he would have been fully familiar with the speech and manners of the kings, princes, noblemen and gallants that feature again and again in the plays.

– Having spent a considerable amount of time in France in his youth, he was fully conversant with the French language, which the author of the plays of Shakespeare knew so well that he was even able, in one scene in the play *Henry V*, to include French slang in it.

– It is on record that, between them, he and his supposed brother Anthony – who in addition to being "related" to him, was also a close friend of his – had travelled to both Scotland and all the places in Europe that the author of the plays must have been well acquainted with in order to depict them as accurately as he did.

– It is no wonder that Shaksper left no mention of any books or entitlement to the revenues from his plays in his will, or ever in his life claimed authorship of the plays.

– It is also no wonder that no reference to such a notable author was made on his death by any of the other literary figures of the day.

– The "impossible" mystery about how it could be that neither the father nor the two surviving children, Susanna and Judith, of one of the greatest and most learned literary figures in history could not read or write, and that there is no specimen of any kind of Shaksper's handwriting in existence, is a mystery no longer.

When, during the period of his known life, would Bacon have written the plays, which would have been, to say the very least, a time-consuming task? An author, Edward D. Johnson, who with much thorough research satisfied himself that "Shakespeare" was Francis Bacon, came up with the following convincing answer, which he included in his book that he wrote, *The Shaksper Illusion*.

As is known, from the time that Francis Bacon was eighteen years old and had returned to England from France, he had ample time for literary work, in whatever quantity. He was a qualified barrister, but never made any appearance in the law courts to argue a case. He was also a Member of Parliament, which, however, was not a time-consuming occupation. For sixteen years he resided in Gray's Inn, with little literary work published under his own name.

On the face of it, all that he produced until, in 1605, he had reached forty-five years of age and *The Advancement of Learning* was published, was a small volume of essays. Was this highly intelligent, well educated and industrious person doing nothing else during that time?

The above-mentioned Edward Johnson believed that Francis Bacon was in fact at that time writing plays that were being publicly performed, and that it was his original intention that all of them should go down to posterity as anonymous productions. Certainly all of the earliest plays – such as *The Taming of the Shrew*, *King Henry VI* in its three parts, *King Richard the Third*, *Romeo and Juliet*, and *King Richard the Second* – were originally published anonymously.

(For the sake of good order in my treatment of this important subject, it is perhaps as well that I mention here that the actual date of first publication of most of the plays is a matter of dispute among scholars, with its being accepted by everyone that complete certainty is impossible. I am using the order, and in the next paragraph the dating, given by Edward Johnson.)

1597 marked the appearance of the last of the plays to be published anonymously, *King Richard the Second*. This play, in its plot, was an attack on what was to be officially called the Divine Right of Kings, a political principle that had been accepted as valid by all Christians since the dawn of Christian history. Queen Elizabeth at once denounced it as treasonable, and set about trying to find out who the author was so that she could have him brought to the rack. In the following year, 1598, a new edition of *King Richard the Second* was published, with, on the title-page, "William Shake-Speare" shown as its author.

Spelt like that, the name is an obvious pseudonym, and a clever one. It is derived from the Greek goddess Pallas Athene; and not only does the Greek word παλλω (pallo) mean "I shake", but the goddess is always represented in statues with a spear in her hand. Furthermore, she was the patroness of learning, so that the clear implication would be that the purpose of the author was to "shake his spear" at ignorance.

By then, Johnson continues, Bacon, involved as he was in the acting world, had come across an actor called Will Shaksper, who had come to London from Stratford; and he had entered into a financial arrangement with him under which Shaksper would return to Stratford with the agreement to have his name used as a

162

"mask" in exchange for a suitable financial consideration that would enable him to buy a property there.

What is certain is:

that Shaksper *did* return to Stratford, and that he spent the rest of his life there;

that he *did* take with him enough money to pay for the substantial property that he at once bought;

that neither in his will nor in any other published document did this Will Shaksper claim to be the author of the plays;

and that, as already mentioned, Shaksper's death was followed – "impossibly" – by further plays written under his name and also by some of the older plays being revised and added to.

Before we leave Shakespeare and Shaksper, I offer two facts which, taken together, are surely conclusive in the support that they give to Mrs. Gallup's findings.

Fact number one part one. Shakespeare's historical plays proceed in a continuous chronological stream from *King John* to *Henry VIII* with *only one significant gap* in the sequence of kings who give their names to his plays. This gap – this single gap – consists of there being no play about King Henry VII. (There is admittedly no Shakespeare play titled *Edward IV* either, but that cannot be considered a gap, since the whole of King Edward IV's reign was included in the play *Richard III.*)

Fact number one part two. Francis Bacon wrote but a single historical work. Its title? As my readers are perhaps expecting from the manner in which I have led up to it: *The Historie of the Raigne of King Henry VII.*

Most tellingly, moreover, that work of history by Bacon

(a) opens at the *precise* moment of time that Shakespeare's *King Richard the Third* closes: with the death of King Richard at Bosworth on page 1, and, three pages later, with Henry Tudor's immediate assumption of the kingship and, in the battlefield, his being crowned as King Henry VII, with King Richard's crown;

163

and

(b) closes with a hymn of almost unqualified praise of this king, whose nastiness and whose ruthless persecution of his subjects were, as we have seen, of a degree that it would be difficult to exaggerate.

Can it reasonably be doubted that Francis Bacon was sending a signal, an *unmistakable* signal, to future generations? – and that he was enjoying doing so?

I go further. Spelling out even more clearly the relevant facts and the conclusion that they clearly lead to:

   – On the one hand, we have plays by William Shakespeare continuing chronologically from King Richard II to King Henry VIII with *just a single gap* in the sequence, that of King Henry VII.

   – On the other hand, we have the writing of a *single* historical work by Francis Bacon, dealing with the reign of the "missing" King Henry VII,

     and *opening* at the *precise moment of time* that Shakespeare brings his *King Richard III* to an end.

In my submission, the possibility that it could be a random coincidence that Bacon's biography of King Henry VII fits *so exactly* into the single gap left by Shakespeare in his plays is a possibility that is, quite simply, non-existent. The reality now, therefore, is that, even with that evidence on its own, and if there were no other evidence pointing in the same direction, *we have already arrived at a complete, manifest, solidly-proved certainty that the works of Shakespeare were written by Francis Bacon.*

Pause for as long as you would like to, good reader, so as to give your fullest consideration to what I have just put before you in that last paragraph...

To those of us who are both open-minded and reasonably alert once put on enquiry, I do not see how Francis Bacon could have given a clearer signal. Do you?

       *   *   *   *   *

Two paragraphs back I said: "...and if there were no other evidence pointing in the same direction." As we are now about to see, there is in fact *an abundance* of additional evidence. I now return to the facts referred to on page 164, of which so far only the first of them, which I labelled *Fact number one*, has been addressed. As in the case of *Fact number one*, I have divided *Fact number two*, which we are now about to look at, into two parts.

Fact number two part one. In 1599 Francis Bacon was thrown into prison as a result of falling into debt to a Jewish moneylender. He was rescued by his brother Anthony Bacon, who mortgaged his own property and borrowed money in order to pay off his elder brother's debts.

Fact number two part two. In 1600, which was *the very next year*, William Shakespeare's *The Merchant of Venice* was published. In this play there was a character called Antonio, which of course is the Italian version of the name "Anthony", and Antonio behaves exactly as Anthony Bacon had done, pledging his property to help his friend Bassanio to get out of the clutches of the Jewish moneylender Shylock. Would it be unreasonable, furthermore, to wonder if it is a coincidence that the name Bassanio has a very definite similarity to the name Bacon?

*   *   *   *   *

Of all that has appeared in this chapter so far, there is one thing that I for one rejoice over. This is simply that, having started with Francis Bacon as our first possible candidate for the title of the real author who wrote under the pseudonym, William Shakespeare, we need go no further in that part of our investigation.

That is to say: thanks to the help that Mrs. Gallup has given us, we have no need to look at the claims made on behalf of any of the other many candidates; not even those on behalf of Edward de Vere, Christopher Marlowe, the Earl of Derby, Sir Walter Raleigh, and John Donne, let alone the dozens of others that featured in the lists set out in chapter 1 of this PART II. That is further to say: a happy result of looking at the most widely-supported candidate first has been to save me from having to write, and my readers from having to read, additional pages in this book that would have been needed if we had not arrived at the answer to the author-question at this early stage in our search.

Chapter 12
Finalising the rounding-off of the authorship case.

What of the other names that, if we believe Mrs. Gallup's offering, were *also* masks used by Francis Bacon?

Much of the information that now follows, most of it very much summarised, is taken from an exceptionally useful book, *Tudor Problems* by Parker Woodward, that was first published in 1912, by the London publishers Gay and Hancock. I thought it nec-essary to include the information for the sake of reasonable completeness on what is obviously an obviously important aspect of our subject-matter, but I shall not find it at all objectionable if some readers wish to scamper through it rather cursorily.

Edmund Spenser (1592-1598/9).

Edmund Spenser is widely revered as one of the founders of modern English verse. (By "modern English verse", I am not of course referring to what most people today, in accordance with today's standards of versifying, would include as modern English verse. I mean verse (a) that consists of regular lines, each line divided into what are called feet, sometimes five feet, such lines being known as pentameters, and sometimes six feet, hexameters, and (b) in which sometimes words at the end of lines rhyme with words at the end of other lines.)

Spenser wrote ten books in verse, including *The Faerie Queene*, and one book in prose.

He was an English official in Ireland, of no prominence, who spent eighteen years there. Most of the poems attributed to him are dedicated to the ladies of Queen Elizabeth's Court, and yet there is no written correspondence in existence between him and those ladies to show that he was acquainted with any of them. Far from his poetry being incompatible with the view that it was written by the person who wrote the works of Shakespeare, it is, for instance, full of legal technical terms that only an experienced lawyer would have at his command.

Lest anyone should doubt me, here are some examples from Spenser's *Faerie Queene*, with the legal technical terms italicised:

Faerie Queene I. 2:

"And her knights s*ervice* ought *to hold of* her in fee."

"The damsel was attacht and shortly brought

Unto the bar whereat she was arraigned."

Faerie Queene III. 1:

"How can they do so justly?

Doth not the *act* of the parent in any *lawful grant or conveyance bind his heirs*?"

Spenser also showed himself to be acquainted with the writings of Homer, Plato, Plutarch, Virgil, Petrarch, Dante, Ariosto, Boccaccio and Tasso.

Christopher Marlowe (1563/4-1593).

Marlowe, one of most-admired of the Elizabethan playwrights was born in 1563, educated at Cambridge, and killed in a drunken brawl in 1593, at the age of thirty. Remarkably, if he was the author of the plays attributed to him, no play stated as having been written by Marlowe was printed *until after his death*. Attributed to him are:

six plays, including *Dido, Queen of Carthage, Doctor Faustus, Tamburlane* and *The Jew of Malta*, which were the first plays ever to be written in English in the blank verse that became a standard format from then on;

a set of verses titled *Hero and Leander* on a classical theme;

a translation of part of the Roman poet Lucan's *Pharsalia*;

and a translation of part of the Roman poet Ovid's elegy titled *Amores*.

According to Parker Woodward, Marlowe showed himself in his writings to be acquainted with the works of Virgil, Lucan, Ovid, Aristotle, Musaeus, Xenophon, Catullus, Euripides, Herodotus, Hollinshed and Machiavelli.

Certainly the poetry of his plays is similar enough to that of Shakespeare's for it to be reasonable to consider those plays to be by the same author when he was less mature and therefore less skilled at his craft.

Thomas Kyd sometimes known as *Thomas Kidd* (1558-1595).

Nothing of significance is known about him other than that he was educated at Merchant Taylor's School. We do not even know if he went to university, and, since there is no record of his having done so, it must be unlikely that he did.

Attributed to him are a few plays for which he never claimed authorship, the most noteworthy of which is *The Spanish Tragedie*. Some people think him to have been only their part-author.

According to Parker Woodward once again, he was well-acquainted with the works of Ovid, Plato, Virgil, Catullus, Cicero, Lucan, Aesop, Claudian, Seneca, Petrarch, Tasso and Machiavelli

Thomas Nashe (1567-1601).

He was educated at Cambridge, and attributed to him are a number of pamphlets, a single piece of theatre, *Summer's Last Will and Testament*, a satire, *Pierce Penniless,* and a few other works. Strangely, his name appears on the title-page of Christopher Marlowe's *Dido, Queen of Carthage*, without any indication of what he contributed to that publication.

He showed himself to have been familiar with the writings of Plutarch, Pliny, Ovid, Tully, Tasso, Aesop, Seneca, Erasmus, Chaucer and Gower.

Stephen Gosson.

Born in 1554 and educated at Oxford, Gosson is said to have been an actor, though no details of his acting career survive. At the age of about thirty, he took holy orders, and soon afterwards was given a rectory to live in by Queen Elizabeth. Strangely, there is no record of his ever having made any claim to the authorship of works published in his name.

Attributed to him is a pamphlet titled *Schoole of Abuse, containing a pleasant invective against Poets, Pipers, Plaiers, Jesters and such like Caterpillars of the Commonwealth* and a second tract, *The Ephemerides of Phialo, and A Short Apologie of the Schoole of Abuse*, both published in 1579. The two are commonly described as euphuistic in nature, the word "euphuism" being derived from the best-known work of the contemporary author or supposed author John Lyly, whom we shall be meeting shortly.

Astonishingly, Gosson shows himself to be acquainted with the works of all of the following: the classical poets Homer, Ovid, Simonides, Pindar, Virgil, Lucan and Ennius; the Bible's theologians Solomon and David; the classical philosophers Plato, Aristotle, Pythagoras, Aurelius and Demosthenes, Cicero, Maximus Tyrius and Hesodius; the historians Sallust, Plutarch, Xenophon, Dion, Julius Caesar and Pliny; and the dramatists Plautus, Seneca, Meander and Euripides.

The cipher story does not expressly mention him by name, but it does refer to the occasional use of – in the story's words – "other names" in addition to those actually mentioned, and Parker Woodward makes this telling point:

> The *Schoole of Abuse* is written very closely in in the style of the *Euphues* of "Lyly". It is passing strange, if indeed not inconceivable, that two writers *in the same year* and in, as it were, the "first fruits" of their respective "inventions" should possess and practise a new and antithetical [contrasting] style, subsequently known as Euphuism. *But*, if one author only was making under two "vizards" [masks], the cause for wonder of course ends.

Not the least remarkable feature of Gosson in this context is that, although he lived to the age of sixty-nine, he stopped writing at the age of twenty-seven. It would be difficult to think of any other instance of such a career as an author.

He never made any claim to authorship, incidentally.

Henry Willobie and *Hadrian Dorrell* (dates of birth and death unknown in both cases).

All that is on record about either of them is that Henry Willobie, sometimes Willoughby, is the supposed author of a "novella" in English verse titled *Willobie His Avisa* published in 1594 and a second edition of which was published by a Hadrian Dorrell, together with an "Apologie" added by Dorrell.

There is no other trace of the existence of Dorrell, and a number of people have suggested that Shakespeare may in some way be connected with *Willobie His Avisa*. In Parker Woodward's words, he, Dorrell, "knew the law extremely well," as also he knew Homer, Plato, Aristotle, Pinda, Plutarch, Eusebius, Ariosto, More, Sidney, Spenser and the Bible.

Robert Burton (1577-1640).

He was educated at Oxford University and spent most of his life there. His most famous work, and indeed the only work that seems to be attributed to him is *Anatomy of Melancholy* by "Democritus Junior", a massive book of 855 pages, and containing in it "the basics" of the novel, *New Atlantis*, that Francis Bacon was later to write.

John Lyly (1553/1554-1569).

Possibly educated at Oxford. He was befriended by the Lord Burghley of that period and in due course became the private secretary of Burghley's son-in-law Edward de Vere, 17th Earl of Oxford, who was himself a playwright and to whom the second part of Lyly's best-known work *Euphues: The Anatomy of Wit*, a so-called prose romance and published in 1578, is dedicated. That work, which was followed by *Euphues and His England* in 1580, gave rise to the introduction of the term "euphuism" into the English language, its meaning being a strange, "mannered", and ornate style that made excessive use of literary devices such as antitheses, alliterations, repetitions and purely rhetorical questions.

He is said, following that, to have taken up the writing of plays; and these are attributed to him: *Campaspe* (published in quarto form in 1584), *Sapho and Phao* (also in 1584), *Endymion* (1591), *Gallathea* (1592), *Midas* (1592), *Mother Bombie* (1594), *The Woman in the Moon (1597)* and *Love's Metamorphosis* (1601).

Here is what the famous 1911 edition of the *Encyclopaedia Britannica* has to say in its entry on John Lyly:

> It [Lyly's dialogue] represents an important step in English dramatic art. His nimbleness, and the wit which struggles with his pedantry, found their full development in the dialogue of Twelfth Night and Much Ado about Nothing, just as "Marlowe's mighty line" led up to and was eclipsed by the majesty and music of Shakespearian passion.

That, of course, is consistent with the author of "Shakespeare" having written earlier plays under the name of Lyly, when his skills at composition were less advanced than they were to become.

In the two *Euphues* works, the author displayed extensive classical learning that included familiarity with the works of Pliny, Plutarch, Plato, Aristotle, Ovid, Cicero, Pythagoras and Anaxagoras.

Thomas Watson (no dates of either his birth or his death are indicated anywhere).

Parker Woodward, on page 100 of his *Tudor Problems* (Gay and Hancock, London, 1912), unhesitatingly describes Watson as "a biographical myth", and goes on to say:

> Nothing is known of him. His supposed biography has been compiled merely by inferences from the writings printed with his name as author... The first "Watson" publication was in 1581 and consisted of a translation from Greek into Latin of the theatrical tragedy *Antigone*, by Sophocles.

Together with a few Latin poems and four Themata, thus called – themes expressed in verse – he produced, after the *Antigone* translation, about a hundred poems in sonnet form, in which he shows himself to be acquainted with a contemporary *French* poet,

Ronsard, a few current Italian poets, and also with (a) the Greek writers Theocritus, Sophocles, Musaeus, Aristotle, Homer and Apollonius, and (b) the Latin authors Ovid, Cicero, Lucan, Seneca, Horace, Pliny, Martial and Flaccus. After offering copious further evidence, including, in his words, "internal evidence consisting of several distinctly Baconian phrases in the Watson writings", Woodward concludes on page 107:

> The "Watson" writings are very evidently the work of Francis Bacon – much of it early work but nonetheless important.

George Peele (1558-1598).

After his schooling at Christ's Hospital, Peele was educated at Christchurch Oxford from 1571 until he graduated as MA in 1579. In 1581 he was married and settled in London, where, in 1583, he arranged the production of two Latin plays. According to Parker Woodward, the bilateral cipher story states that, for payment in money, he sold to Francis Bacon the use of his name as the supposed author of certain of Bacon's plays and verses.

Of those the plays consist of:

The Arraignment of Paris: a Pastoral Presented before the Queen's Majestie published anonymously in 1584.

Edward I, published under the name of George Peele in 1593.

The love of King David and Fair Bethsabe with the tragedy of Absalom, published under the name of George Peele in 1599

The Old Wives' Tale published under the name G. P. In 1595.

He also wrote a number of poetical works, and Parker Woodward ends his chapter on him thus:

> The Peele writings show that the author was acquainted with the works of Vergil, Pliny, Horace, Juvenal, Cicero, Plautus, Ariosto, du Bartas, Chaucer, Gower and Holinshed. A careful comparison of the acts and life of Peele as known to us together with the plays and verses ascribed to him, and a study of the internal evidence, fully support the assertion of

the cipher-story that the works in the name of Peele were written by Bacon.

Robert Greene (1558-1592).

He was a professional actor. Attributed to him are the following plays, which I give together with the dates on which they were first published: *Selimus* (1594); *Orlando Furioso* (1594); *Looking Glass For London* (1594); *Friar Bacon* (1594); *Alphonsus, King of Aragon* (1597); *James IV of Scotland* (1598); *Pinner of Wakefield* (1599).

According to Parker Woodward, one literary critic, Professor Brown, went so far as to say that *James IV of Scotland* "is the finest Elizabethan historical play outside Shakespeare, and worth to be placed on a level with Shakespeare's earlier style", and indeed that in style "Greene is the father of Shakespeare." Woodward then adds:

> M. Jusserand, writing about Greene, states: "Learned he was, versed in the Greek, Latin, French and Italian tongues."

"*So was Francis Bacon*," is Woodward's comment that immediately follows that. (The italics are his.)

William Webbe (dates of birth and death unknown)

Attributed to him is a booklet *Discourse of English Poetrie*, first published in 1586, and which, according to Parker Woodward on page 189 of his book, "can be safely added to his [Francis Bacon's] authorship credit." To support this he gives examples of what he calls "internal evidence" of Baconian authorship, such as the use of the term "merry tales" that is also found in Bacon's *Promus* and the treatment of the Orpheus legend in the same way as Bacon treats it in his *Wisdom of the Ancients*, and, perhaps most convincing of all, anticipates "Shakespeare" in dividing his plays into Comedies, Tragedies and Histories and also in other respects. Even more tellingly, a play that was published in 1592, *Tancred and Gismunda*, included an Introduction supposedly written by Webbe, which, says Woodward,

...betrays that its writer was a lawyer, whose mind was saturated with legal jargon – a mind that in fact was the mind of Francis Bacon at the age of thirty-two.

For instance, the words and phrases "respite", "arrest", "*actum est*", "case", "judge's court", "charges", "action", "cause", "plead" and "parties" appear in the first few sentences.

At this point Woodward concludes:

We affirm with confidence that "Webbe" was only a cover for Francis Bacon, the true author of the Discourse.

Chapter 13
Yet another significant literary production.

Worth mentioning as a possibility, which I offer to readers who would prefer to be aware rather than unaware of it, some people – including a few past members of the Francis Bacon Society that was founded in 1886 and whose members are for the most part admirers of Bacon – have thought that Bacon was the translator of the King James Version of the Bible, which was for centuries the official Bible used by the Church of England.

How likely, it is certainly worth asking, is it that this is so?

A fair number of things are worth drawing attention to in relation to this suggested possibility, one of which I class as being as spectacular, in its remarkableness, as anything mentioned in this book.

The first and perhaps most important of these is that the King James Version is justly rated as, in the beauty of its language, one of the finest examples of prose ever written in English, an inspiration to generations of writers all kinds, and even to artists and musicians. It is by far the most famous of the translations into English of the Bible, and many of the phrases in it have become part of the very fabric of the English language. Here are some examples:

"A broken heart" (Psalms 34:18), "A labour of love" (Hebrews 6:10), "A law unto themselves" (Romans 2:14), "A stumbling block" (Romans 14:13), "A thorn in the flesh" (II Corinthians 12:7), "All things to all men" (1 Corinthians 9:22), "At their wits' end" (Psalm 107:27), "Bite the dust" (Psalms 2:9), "By their fruits ye shall know them" (Matthew 7:16), "By the skin of your teeth" (Job 19,20), "A leopard cannot change its spots" (Jeremiah 13:23), "Cast the first stone" (John 8:7), "Eat, drink and be merry" (Ecclesiastes 8:15), "Fallen from grace" (Galatians 5;4), "Fell by the wayside" (Luke 8:5), "Fell flat on his face" (Numbers 2:21), "Fell on stony ground" (Mark 4:5), "For everything there is a season" (Ecclesiastes 3:1), "Go from strength to strength" (Psalm 84:7), "God forbid" (Romans 6:2), "How are the mighty fallen" (Samuel 1:19), "In the twinkling of an eye" (1 Corinthians 15:52), "Put words in[to] your mouth" (Isaiah 51:16), "Signs of the times" (Matthew 16:3), "Suffer fools gladly" (2 Corinthians 11:19), "Teeth set on edge" (Jeremiah 31:29), "The blind leading the blind" (Matthew 15: 13,14), "The land of the living" (Psalm 27:13), "The powers that be" (Romans 13:1), "The root of the matter" (Job 19:28), "To take root" (Isaiah 27:6), "Turned the world upside-down" (Acts 17:6), "Vengeance is mine" (Romans 12:13), "Weighed in the balance" (Job 31:6) ,"Woe is me" (Isaiah 6:5)...

I could go on and on; and I stress that, although I have thought it worth giving quite a large number of examples in order to provide a reasonable indication of the King James Version's effect on the English language, the collection above is nowhere near to being a complete one. Even taking into account the fact of the translator or translators having had wonderful material to work with, the translating was powerful writing by whichever author or authors was or were responsible.

In the light of what we are considering in this book, it is certainly worth asking ourselves who indeed was responsible for the extraordinary achievement that is the King James Version.

What we are officially told, and as has always been believed by most people who have addressed the matter, is that the translation was put together by a group of no fewer than forty-seven writers working together, who were Church of England scholars commissioned for this purpose by King James I and who brought the task to completion in 1611.

This account of its origin, although generally accepted, in fact has only to be thought about for a few seconds for it to be seen to be impossible. Good writing has never been done in that way and never could be, let alone writing that is not merely good but outstanding in its quality, as in this case. High quality writing is done:

(a) almost exclusively by highly talented *individuals*, for the most part working alone; (b) very occasionally by two people writing together (as in the case of the ladies Somerville and Ross); and (c) never by a greater number of authors than that.

Add to that the fact that Francis Bacon had a close relationship with James I, whom, as we have seen, he served at different times as Attorney General and as Lord Chancellor of England, and the possibility that he was the translator of the King James Version has clearly lost some of its non-credibility.

What, however, we may ask ourselves, would have motivated Francis Bacon, who seems to have been morally perverted in a number of ways, to devote much time and energy to making as accessible as reasonably possible the literary work that was reckoned to be the Divinely-inspired-in-every-detail word of God?

Sadly, the likely answer to that question is all too clear and all too painful. Another notable feature of the King James Version, this one horrifying for those who believe the Bible to be the word of God, and inspired in every detail by the Holy Ghost, is that it contains mistranslations that cannot possibly be mere slips, and in some cases are – I do not exaggerate – really *gross* mistranslations, drastically falsifying the meaning of the original.

I have just used the word "gross" and I really believe that to be appropriate, given the clear realities just referred to:

(a) that the mistranslations include ones that are, genuinely, starkly *in opposition to* the meaning of the originals,

and

(b) that so *obviously* are they such extreme mistranslations that they could not possibly be accidental.

For our present purposes, I shall offer for assessment by my readers just two such falsifications of the original text, both of them clear and also horrifyingly perverse.

For my first example, here is verse 14 of chapter 2 of the New Testament's *Gospel According to Saint Luke*. Correctly translated, whether from the original Greek or from the later Latin version of the Bible, known as the Vulgate, which was a direct translation of the original Greek, this reads:

Glory to God in the highest; and on Earth peace to men of goodwill.

Here, for the benefit of any of my readers who have some competence in classical Greek or Biblical Greek, is the original Greek from which that was translated:

Δόξα ἐν ὑψίστοις Θεῷ καὶ ἐπὶ γῆς εἰρήνη ἐν ἀνθρώποις εὐδοκίας.

Here, too. is the Latin translation of that Greek sentence, in the Vulgate

Gloria in altissimis Deo et in terra pax in hominibus bonae voluntatis.

Here, finally, is the King James Version's rendering of it, mistranslating and shamelessly misrepresenting the original:

Glory to God in the highest, and on earth *peace* [and] *good will toward men.*

Spelling it out:

(a) In the Greek and the Latin, the wish for peace and good will is strictly limited *only* to those of goodwill;

(b) In the New King James translation, the wish for peace and good is *universal.*

As anyone with sufficient knowledge of either or both of Classical Greek and Latin can confirm, the original is so elementary and straightforward that even the veriest beginner among learners of Greek would not get that translation wrong.

The same applies to the second example that I now offer, the fourth verse of chapter 2 of the *Gospel According to Saint John.* Here, first, is the literal translation of both the Greek and the Latin:

And Jesus saith/said to her: Woman, what is that to me and to thee? My hour /time is not yet come.

The King James Version translation of that is:

Jesus saith unto her, Woman, what have I to do with thee? Mine hour is not yet come.

The original Greek is:

Καὶ λέγει αὐτῇ ὁ Ἰησοῦς: Τί ἐμοὶ καὶ σοί, γύναι; οὔπω ἥκει ἡ ὥρα μου.

Before moving on to the Latin version of that, I should make it clear that the tenth word of that sentence, the noun γυνή, of which the word γύναι there is the vocative singular case, is not offensive in Greek, as the translation, "woman", might be in English. "Lady" or "Madam" is closer to the sense in that context.

Here is the same sentence in the Vulgate's Latin translation of the original Greek, word for word as in the English above:

Et dicit ei Jesus: Quid mihi et tibi est, mulier? nondum venit hora mea.

The difference between the King James Version and the original could hardly be more different. In the original Jesus is *uniting* Himself with His mother "…to me *and* to thee". In the mistranslation, He is *separating* Himself from her, dramatically and even insultingly.

I could offer more examples, but those two are so clear-cut and so dramatic, arguably even startling, in their nature that they are surely sufficient to show:

first, that the King James Version is not remotely to be trusted as being what it is believed to be by those who are devoted to it,

and secondly, that such mistranslating is far from neutral in its effects and in its presentation of the message contained in those verses.

Indeed it is so far from neutral as actually to distort the meaning *damagingly* and even grossly so, and of course especially in the second one, where Jesus, when He is in reality *uniting Himself* with Mary, is represented as *separating Himself* from her, and in a disparaging way.

Oh my goodness! What Bacon did in those pages may seem inoffensive to some in the modern world, but, at the time that he was working on the King James Version, the contents of the

Bible, regarded as "the Word of God", were considered to be so sacrosanct that few crimes were held in lower esteem than misrepresenting it or in any other way distorting or damaging it. From what we now know of Francis Bacon, however, it would of course have been something of a surprise to us if any involvement by him with the King James Version had been *without* harmful consequences. What we could rightly expect is what we have indeed got. Some of my readers might feel like joining me in saying, justifiably:

Like rotten mackerel in the moonlight, he shines and he stinks.

We are not yet *quite* ready to leave this important subject of Bacon and the Bible and to move on. What is now to come is an unmistakable signal that Bacon included in the King James Version, as a sort of joke to make it clear who the translator was to those who kept their wits about them. Are you ready, good reader, for yet another of the "extraordinaries" that I am able to fill these pages with?

If you can get access to the King James Version, as can be done, for instance by doing a word-search for "King James Version" in the Internet, and then turn to Psalm 46 there, you will find that it consists, in total, of the following, in which, as you will see, as you look through it, I have highlighted in capital letters two of its words, one in verse 3 and the other in verse 9.

1. God is our refuge and strength, a very present help in trouble.

2. Therefore will not we fear, though the earth be removed, and though the mountains be carried into the midst of the sea;

3. Though the waters thereof roar and be troubled, though the mountains SHAKE with the swelling thereof.

4. There is a river, the streams whereof shall make glad the city of God, the holy place of the tabernacles of the most High.

5. God is in the midst of her; she shall not be moved: God shall help her, and that right early.

6. The heathen raged, the kingdoms were moved: he uttered his voice, the earth melted.

7. The Lord of hosts is with us; the God of Jacob is our refuge.

8. Come, behold the works of the Lord, what desolations he hath made in the earth.

9. He maketh wars to cease unto the end of the earth; he breaketh the bow, and cutteth the SPEAR in sunder; he burneth the chariot in the fire.

10. Be still, and know that I am God: I will be exalted among the heathen, I will be exalted in the earth.

11. The Lord of hosts is with us; the God of Jacob is our refuge.

What, in the above, is of interest, to say the least, is that, in that Psalm 46, the 46th word from the beginning, which occurs in verse 3, is "shake", and the 46th word from the end is "spear".

As we have learnt, Bacon believed in giving signals, and here he was clearly sending one, and was amusing himself as he did so. This is of course not unreasonable *as such*, if there are no other considerations to take into account. Messing about with the *Bible* is a different matter, however. I do not believe that we can consider this particular display of his brilliance – involving as it did playing "clever-clever" with the book regarded by countless millions over the centuries as inspired by the God who created the universe and each of us individuals in it – to be either culturally or morally acceptable.

*   *   *   *   *

What else can usefully be said about this in every way extraordinary man of prodigious genius that was Francis Bacon?

To his great credit, he was, as we have seen, more than anyone else responsible for the English language being transformed from a language that for much of its history had been looked down on and scarcely used as a medium for writing in into one of the three great languages of Europe in history, the other two being classical Greek and classical Latin.

Be assured that this was an extraordinary achievement. Soon after the time of Geoffrey Chaucer in the Fifteenth Century, English had ceased to be used as a language for any kind of serious writing. Latin had replaced it as the preferred language for that purpose, as in fact had been the norm even in Chaucer's era.

It is indeed no exaggeration to say that modern English as we know it actually started to come into existence with the appearance of Spenser's *The Faerie Queen* and then "took off" with the writings labelled with the names of Marlowe, Kyd, Nashe, Gosson and the rest, including of course Shakespeare.

The lowest number of words that Bacon is thought to have added to the English vocabulary is one thousand seven hundred, but some experts in such matters have estimated the real number at between five thousand and six thousand.

It is largely due to him that, for most concepts expressed in English, there are at least two different words with basically the same meanings but subtly different *shades* of meaning, one of them – the first of them chronologically – based on an original Anglo-Saxon word and the other being a Latin-derived word. Examples are "have" and "possess", "be" and "exist", "help" and "assist", "buy" and "purchase", "try" and "endeavour", "seller" and "vendor", "giver" and "donor", "need" and "necessity", "loving" and "amorous", "thankful" and "grateful"; and "want" and "desire".

Another significant contribution of his to the world of his day and thereafter right up to the present day is that, whether to his credit or otherwise, he is officially acknowledged by the Royal Society, the oldest and most distinguished scientific society in the world, to have been, with his book, *New Atlantis*, that was published in 1627, very probably the leading inspiration that led to founding of that institution.

"Whether to his credit or otherwise," I have just said. I perhaps owe it to my readers to set down a few basic facts about this book, *New Atlantis*, in case they would like some help in forming an opinion of which of the two alternatives I have put forward – either "to his credit" or "otherwise" – is the case. *New Atlantis* is what is technically called a philosophical novel; in other words, by no means written purely for the entertainment of its readers. Under that heading, it is commonly described as utopian, Utopia being an imagined community with a perfect political and social system and whose citizens possess the most desirable qualities.

In this book, Bacon presented a vision of human discovery and knowledge that would take place in the future, expressing his aspirations and ideals for humankind and depicting a mythical and utopian land, Bensalem, where "generosity and enlightenment, dignity and splendour, piety and public spirit" are the commonly held qualities of its inhabitants. Often referred to as "a work of Utopian magic realism" – magic realism being a technical term for works of literature, and especially of fiction, that combine a realistic view of the world with magic (which means *black* magic) elements – it is thought by many to be a genuinely sinister book.

I hope that my readers, or at least many of them, are starting to see reasons to feel uncomfortable about Francis Bacon. Sadly, I must add further reasons.

Very much *not* to his credit, he undoubtedly involved himself heavily in the occult and esoteric, and was deeply secretive, not only about his authorships, as of course we have been learning, but about much else as well. I suggest that this alone should be sufficient to make us deeply suspicious of him in general. Keeping any significant activities that one engages in carefully concealed is almost always going to be for reasons ranging from bad to profoundly sinister, both in one's motives and in one's character.

It would perhaps be surprising if Bacon were otherwise in his character. As mentioned earlier, his real mother was closely involved with the magician Dr. John Dee, and he, Francis Bacon, would therefore certainly have known him well.

Also of interest, it has been thought by a number of scholarly authors – indeed even certain by some – that Bacon was the founder of the two most prominent secret societies, the Freemasons and the Rosicrucians.

The officially-recognised start-up date of the Freemasons is 1717, but what in fact happened then was that a "grand lodge" was formed in London in order to be the head of a number of lodges that *already* existed. As to those lodges, there are no definite records of their origins, and in particular there are no records of the coming into existence of the rituals, which, whatever else may be said about them, are examples of singularly beautiful English, of a definite "Shakespearean" kind – and of which Bacon, therefore, could well have been the author.

The Rosicrucians started earlier than the Freemasons but gradually and progressively faded away until, as recently as in the mid-19th-century, they suddenly took off again, first in the United States. Their earliest surviving rituals too are in beautiful English, and it is not known who originally composed them,

Since my readers may include members of one or other or both of those societies, I shall not embark on any sort of *detailed* discussion on them. Two points are certainly important enough to be worth noting here, however.

One is that both Freemasons and Rosicrucians have what are called "Degrees" of membership, several such Degrees in each case,

In the case of Freemasonry, for instance, an incoming member starts as an "Entered Apprentice", or First-Degree member of Freemasonry. He – there are no lady-members – then moves on to the "Fellow Craft" or Second Degree, and then to being a "Master Mason", of the Third Degree. (It is widely supposed, even among Masons when they first join the Order, that Masonic membership-progress stops there, but in fact it continues for many more degrees, in fact thirty-three. For instance, the present – as in the year 2020 – Duke of Kent, who is, as he has been for more than fifty years, what is called the Grand Master of the United Grand Lodge of England, is a thirty-third degree Freemason.)

As to the Rosicrucians, I shall leave it to readers who are interested to do their own research if they care to. Here it is sufficient to note that the basic system of organisation, into Degrees, is the same as that of Freemasonry

The second point worth noting here is that various facts relating to those degrees are hidden from those who are members of lower degrees of the societies in question, those who move up to a higher degree being required to make oaths, of the highest severity, that they will not disclose to anyone, even fellow-members of lower degrees, what they are about to learn in consequence of joining this higher degree.

Outsiders have an undoubted right to be concerned about all this secrecy, and indeed to regard it as a sound reason to refuse invitations to become members; and potential members certainly have been known to refuse to join for that reason.

This is not to assert that the Freemasons and the Rosicrucians are criminal organisations as such. I do maintain, however, that if – and may it not be so! – one were to wish to start up and run a criminal organisation, the most efficient basic form of it would certainly be along Masonic and Rosicrucian lines.

*   *   *   *   *

Time, now to cast a brief look at Francis Bacon's philosophy, the like of which the world had never seen before.

Chapter 14
The revolutionary philosophy founded by the author.

For a start, devastatingly revealing of Francis Bacon's character is *his own view* of his philosophical output. Could anyone else in all history have written as conceitedly about his or her own work as what Bacon wrote in and about his *Novum Organum*? Please read it more than once, good reader. I believe it more than merely possible that you will become the more shocked the more you ponder on it.

The die is cast, the book is written, to be read either now or by posterity – I care not which; it may wait a century for a reader, as God has waited six thousand years for an observer.

*   *   *   *   *

My readers can now breathe a sigh of relief if they trust my judgement; for in this instance it is my judgement is that they do not need to undertake the labour of becoming students of Bacon's philosophy. I take it upon myself:

(a) to class the *Novum Organum* as perverse, pernicious and vile,

and

(b) to assert, moreover, that it can be easily *demonstrated* to be so.

The central principle of Francis Bacon's philosophy, governing all the rest of it, was what he called his Inductive Method. *Induction* must rule, and it must take the place of *deduction*, he insisted.

Up until then, the recognised means of arriving at certain knowledge about anything of even the smallest amount of complexity was the syllogism.

The syllogism? For the benefit of those who have not made a technical study of the process of reasoning, the syllogism is its principal and indispensable tool. It consists of three successive steps: the major premise, the minor premise and the conclusion.

The first step, *the major premise*, is always a *general* statement that is universally true and cannot be otherwise, such as:

"Dogs do not have wings and cannot fly."

The second step, *the minor premise*, is a *particular* statement that is *also* undoubtedly true, such as:

"I am the owner of a dog."

The third step, the *conclusion* is what follows from the two premises when they are correctly put together, in this case:

"Therefore, even if you have never seen my dog, you can be *completely* certain that it has no wings and cannot fly."

Provided that the necessary conditions for each *premise* – that one can be certain (a) that each premise is correct and (b) that they have been correctly combined – are met, the *conclusion* is inescapable.

That is how we do *all* of our thinking, whether we realise it or not. Without syllogisms we cannot reason, and indeed, if anyone should wish to try to prove that syllogisms are unnecessary, he would need to use syllogisms in order to do so.

Bacon's new decree on this subject was:

Deduction and the syllogism must be rejected as unscientific.

Rather, *induction* was the only instrument of philosophy and scientific reasoning that was serviceable.

Induction, he said, proceeds by slow and careful steps. For every act of induction, the scientist must put together long lists of relevant facts, then study them with care, and then arrive at a conclusion based on the direction to which, in their accumulation, these relevant facts point.

*　　*　　*　　*　　*

One can fairly describe that teaching of Bacon's as painful, and indeed, as I suggested a few paragraphs back, in fact worse than merely painful. It is as well that I quote his exact words on the subject, so that readers can judge for themselves. From the introductory chapter of his treatise on philosophy and science, *The Great Instauration*:

In the ordinary logic, almost all the work is spent about the syllogism. Of induction the logicians seem hardly to have taken any serious thought, but they pass it by with a slight notice, and hasten on to the formulae of disputation.

In the first place, that is not merely untrue. In addition, it *cannot* be a mere *error*.

Spelling it out: it can *only* be an actual *lie* on Bacon's part. No one claiming to know enough about traditional philosophy to be able to argue against it could be unaware that induction has been an *indispensable* part of philosophy *right from the beginning*. Indeed one of the many titles of the first of all of the classical philosophers that Bacon was opposing, Socrates, is "The father of induction".

Lest anyone should doubt what I have just said on this important matter of the position of induction in pre-Baconian philosophy, I turn to a typical textbook on traditional philosophy, *An Introduction to Philosophy* by Msgr. Paul J. Glenn (Herder Book Co., St. Luis, U.S.A., 1944). On page 71:

When the reasoning process or syllogism proceeds from individual instances to general or universal conclusion, the process is *inductive reasoning* or simply *induction*. The principle of induction is this: whatever is true of each member of a class is true of all members; whatever is to be denied of each is to be denied of all. Deduction and induction are complementary, not opposed, methods of reasoning.

In the second place, to dismiss syllogistic deduction as useless, as Bacon did, is to make proper reasoning actually *impossible*.

In the third place, insanely, he actually proved what I have just said, under the heading of "In the second place", *by himself using a syllogism* in order to prove, supposedly, that deduction was an invalid and useless process of reasoning.

Lest anyone should, understandably, find it hard to believe that such an intelligent man could *really* have been guilty of such a flagrant internal self-contradiction, here he is in action, later in that paragraph of *The Great Instauration* from which I have just quoted:

The syllogism consists of propositions; propositions of words; and words of the tokens and signs of notions. Now, if the very notions of mine (which are at the soul of words and the bases of the whole structure) be improperly and over-hastily abstracted from facts that are vague, are not sufficiently definite and, in short, are faulty in many ways, the whole edifice tumbles. I therefore reject the syllogism.

The first sentence of that paragraph was the major premise. The second sentence was the minor premise. The third sentence, starting with the words "I therefore", was the conclusion.

Yes, scarcely believably, in his attempt to justify the *rejection* of the syllogism, as part of reasoning, Bacon actually *uses* a syllogism.

The *realities* are (a) that Bacon could not do without the syllogism, and (b) that no one else can either.

What is more, to the extent that people ever *try* to do without the syllogism, what the exclusive use of induction means is that one can never be certain of anything. No matter how many experiments might point, with their results, in a certain direction, one can never be *certain* that the *next* experiment will not point in the *opposite* direction, because a *general* truth is never allowed by Bacon to exist, a *general* truth being the first and *major* premise of a syllogism. According to induction *on its own*:

(a) however many dogs you might have seen that had no wings and could not fly, you could not be sure that the next dog would not be an exception; and, for that matter,

(b) in this book that you are reading, for which I have gone to much trouble to make sure that every judgement in it is true, there cannot be one single sentence presented as a factual judgement that is *definitely* true.

*   *   *   *   *

A few paragraphs back, I asserted that Bacon had not merely been *mistaken* in what he had asserted but had actually *lied* in that instance. It is worth taking a further look at this aspect of Francis Bacon that has suddenly emerged.

The reality is that, since he was – as we know both from his reputation and by what has been shown to be in these pages – one of the most intelligent men who ever lived, and well educated as well, it is simply not realistic to suppose that he was ignorant of the central and indispensable part in thinking that, as I have just been outlining, is played by deduction and the syllogism. From this it follows that he could *only* have been *deliberately* setting out to promote a philosophy that he *knew* to be an invalid one. That in turn means that his purpose was to be destructive.

That is to say, his purpose must have been to eradicate, as far as he could, the ability of mankind to think, to reason, to communicate accurately, and to discuss and debate to good effect. In other words, his purpose must have been to eradicate the abilities of mankind (a) to distinguish truth from falsehood and (b) to be steadfast in pursuit of truth.

That amounted to an attack on civilisation, since civilisation cannot be otherwise than precarious and its continuation is inevitably dependent on the ability of a significant proportion of its members to perceive, promote and defend truth, rightness and even beauty, and everything depending on those fundamentals.

*   *   *   *   *

If we look around us now, it could be argued that Francis Bacon has been all too successful in that endeavour of his. I take just one example, selected because it is both clearly evident, indeed actually visible, and also inescapable in what it shows.

Back in the Middle Ages, there came into existence all over Europe as well as in England, quite suddenly, and as though effortlessly, the mediaeval cathedrals and other important church buildings that were and are – those many that have survived – of such architectural beauty as to have been popular destinations for sightseeing ever since. By contrast, in our era even the most expensive new buildings can fairly be described as eyesores by comparison.

No less important, for our purpose here, is the fact that, even with all the improvements in technology that have been developed since then, buildings such as those cathedrals *could not be built today.*

To explain.

Anyone can design a building which will stand up. That does not take great skill. What *does* take great skill, and in fact is one of the most important skills in the science of architecture, is that of designing buildings which will only *just* stand up, a skill which reaches its peak, and in the case of cathedrals the level of genius, when buildings are designed which, to all appearances, ought *not* to stand up but somehow do, *and* are breathtakingly beautiful as well.

That was the level reached in the Middle Ages, and not only in cathedrals, but in the architecture of abbeys, colleges in the universities of Oxford and Cambridge, and the like, and indeed in buildings of various kinds that are to be found all over England.

All that architectural competence is now gone. I do not claim to have proved that Francis Bacon was responsible for this. I *do* claim to have proved that such, for whatever reason, was his *purpose*. If you doubt that, please remind yourself, if you now accept that he was the author of the phenomenally influential works attributed to Shakespeare, of what his purpose can *only* have been with those works.

Chapter 15
A religious revolutionary as well.

One last topic that needs to be looked at, in order to obtain a reasonably comprehensive picture of Francis Bacon as a teacher-in-action, is what he had to say on the subject of religion. We have already had something of an indirect look at this under the heading of his having probably been the translator of the King James Version of the Bible, and also elsewhere in these pages, and the time has now come for confronting the whole topic of Bacon and Christianity head-on.

If we recollect that there is not a single Christian theme presented anywhere in the works attributed to his *alias*, William Shakespeare, we can think it hardly likely that there will be a traditional treatment of Christianity anywhere *else* in his writings. Nor is there.

Reason, Francis Bacon maintained when he was addressing philosophical matters, could have nothing to do with religion. One's religious beliefs and convictions *must be based on faith alone.*

That belief is of course quite commonly held in our day, but it was revolutionary in his day. For the previous fifteen hundred years the whole *basis* of the traditional Christian position was that it could be *proved* to be the only true religion. There was even a *science*, called apologetics, that was devoted to how that proving could best be done.

Bacon's revolutionary assertion was as insane as anything else that he preached to his readers. What follows from that theory of his, after all, is that one cannot use one's reason to judge the merits of one religious position against another.

Traditionally:

(a) Reason was for establishing whether the teaching of a particular religion could be trusted,

(b) Once that was established, then, and *only* then, could one justify trusting – having rational faith in, strictly in accordance with the standard rules of logic (reasoning) – what the particular religion in question taught.

By contrast, once having abandoned any use of reason, how can anyone distinguish between one religion and another? According to the philosophy promoted by Bacon, you should not give any thought to what you are being asked to believe; rather, you should just believe it blindly.

Does that philosophy of Bacon's make sense, as a *worthy* philosophy, to any of my readers? To those whose answer is "yes", the common-sense response must be: if that is how you conduct yourself intellectually, however, you have no protection against believing in fairies or that the moon is made of cheese, or any other nonsense that you may feel the urge to believe.

And, make no mistake, there *are* people who *do* abuse their intellects to that extent and to such effect.

Bacon, therefore, did not launch a *direct* attack on Christianity. The *name* of that religion remained in being.

The *substance* of that religion, however, did *not* remain in being. Moreover, in his day, and then during the period in which the Reformation was initiated – a time when religion was much more central to society than it is today and indeed was the most important political topic of all – that method of his of attacking it might well have been more effective than a more direct method.

*   *   *   *   *

So much for the man who was the rightful heir to the throne of England and Wales, *and* one of the founders of the mighty British Empire of the future, *and*, both under his own name and under false names, one of the most powerful influences on mankind who ever lived, *and* who was never to be King. I believe that I have shown this influence, both directly and under his "masks", to have been malevolent and destructive in the extreme, and to be continuing to be so.

If that is indeed what I have shown, we may perhaps consider it to be not wholly unexpected, given his ancestry, since: –

On his father's side, he was the son of a man who was probably involved in the murder of his own wife.

On his mother's side:

— He was the son of a woman shamelessly guilty of the worst kind of murder, judicial murder, and on a huge scale.

— He was also the grandson of King Henry VIII, who as we have seen, was a judicial-*mass*-murderer.

— And he was the great-grandson of King Henry VII, another judicial-mass-murderer.

Furthermore, on both his father's and his mother's side, he was conceived in a bigamous relationship between his father and his mother.

Furthermore still, both his father and his mother were closely involved with Dr. John Dee, an occultist who dealt in magic, which in his case means sorcery or black magic.

*   *   *   *   *

The point at which we have now certainly arrived is that Francis Bacon, Viscount St. Albans, and Robert Devereux, Earl of Essex, neither of whom had any children, were the last of the Tudors, with Francis Bacon the very last of them. Surely that was just as well.

Surely, indeed, in the case of Francis Bacon it can justly be said:

Like rotten mackerel in the moonlight, he shone and he stank.

Chapter 16
Oh, and those portraits of William Shakespeare?!

In 1623, the First Folio, as it is commonly called – and the full title of which is *Mr. William Shakespeares* [sic] *Comedies, Histories, & Tragedies* – suddenly appeared.

Exactly how this happened is something of a mystery. Shakespeare (Shaksper) himself *had died seven years earlier*, in 1623, and the Folio does not specify who it was who organised the publication. Appearing just inside the cover, in fact just under the portrait that we shall be examining shortly, the printer is given as Isaac Jaggard and the publisher as Ed. Blount, but of course they were mere technicians in the field of publishing. Others that feature at the beginning are John Heminge and John Condell, in introductory essays addressed to "William Earle of Pembroke, &c." and "Philip Earle of Montgomery, &c." What are *nowhere* indicated are such things as:

– Who it was who put the contents of the massive volume together.

– Who it was who organised the several introductory items at the beginning of it.

– Who it was who introduced, in this published edition, no fewer than *eighteen* plays that (a) had never been attributed to "Shakespeare", (b) had never been published in quarto form or any other form until they appeared in 1623, seven years after Shakespeare's death, in the First Folio, and (c), but for which appearance, half of Shakespeare's plays would have been lost. For the record, these new plays are, in alphabetical order: *All's Well That Ends Well, Antony and Cleopatra, As You Like It, The Comedy of Errors, Coriolanus, Cymbeline, Henry VI Part 1, Henry VIII, Julius Caesar, King John, Macb*th, Measure for Measure, The Taming of the Shrew, The Tempest* and *Timon of Athens.*

Moreover, included in this 1623 First Folio are *new passages in existing plays*, such as the addition of one thousand eight hundred lines to Hamlet. (I am indebted to the earlier-mentioned booklet, published in 1924, *The "Shakespeare" Myth: A Challenge* by Lord Sydenham of Combe and H. C. Crouch, for that last piece of information.)

Also not indicated was who the person was who was responsible for the portrait at the beginning of the Folio's second page, a portrait that, in the first place, was somehow brought into existence several years after the death of Stratford's William Shaksper and, in the second place, is very, very strange, as we shall be seeing.

By no means uninteresting too: we do not know who commissioned either of the two poems by Ben Jonson for placement at the beginning of the Folio.

Here is the first of those two poems. It appears on the very first page, immediately opposite the page on which both the full title of the First Folio and the Droeshout picture – which is in fact an engraving, as we about to learn – appear.

> This Figure that thou here seest put,
> It was for gentle Shakespeare cut,
> Wherein the Graver had a strife
> With nature, to out-doo the life.
> O, could he but have dreamt his wit
> As well in brasse as he hath hit
> His face the print would then surpass
> All that was ever writ in brasse:
> But, since he cannot, Reader, looke
> Not on his picture, but his booke.
>
> Ben Jonson

The second poem, which occupies the fifth and sixth pages after the pages with the title and the Droeshout portrait, is in the words of Professor Schoenbaum on 207 page of his book *William Shakespeare – a Documentary Life* (Clarendon Press, Oxford, 1975), "one of the most admired commendatory poems in the English language"; and it consists of a hundred and twenty lines of the most extravagant praise conceivable.

Could the words "the most extravagant praise conceivable" be at least something of an exaggeration? I believe not, and, by quoting enough of it, about half of it, to give an adequate general *impression* of it, I shall invite my readers to make their own judgement. Please do not feel obliged though, good readers, to read it with painstaking attentiveness. (By contrast with how I reproduced the other piece of verse of his, above, I have modernised some of the spelling.)

To the Memory of My Beloved the Author,
Mr. William Shakespeare.

By Ben Jonson

To draw no envy, Shakespeare, on thy name,
  Am I thus ample to thy book and fame;
While I confess thy writings to be such
  As neither man nor muse can praise too much...
I therefore will begin. Soul of the age!
  The applause, delight, the wonder of our stage!
My Shakespeare, rise! I will not lodge thee by
  Chaucer, or Spenser, or bid Beaumont lie
A little further, to make thee a room:
  Thou art a monument without a tomb,
And art alive still while thy book doth live
  And we have wits to read and praise to give....
And though thou hadst small Latin and less Greek,
  From thence to honour thee, I would not seek
For names; but call forth thund'ring Aeschylus,
  Euripides and Sophocles to us;
Pacuvius, Accius, him of Cordova dead,
  To life again, to hear thy buskin tread,
And shake a stage; or, when thy socks were on,
  Leave thee alone for the comparison
Of all that insolent Greece or haughty Rome
  Sent forth, or since did from their ashes come.
Tri'umph, my Britain, thou hast one to show
  To whom all scenes of Europe homage owe.
He was not of an age but for all time!

And all the Muses still were in their prime,
When, like Apollo, he came forth to warm
    Our ears, or like a Mercury to charm!
Nature herself was proud of his designs
    And joy'd to wear the dressing of his lines,
Which were so richly spun, and woven so fit,
    As, since, she will vouchsafe no other wit.
        ....Look how the father's face
Lives in his issue, even so the race
Of Shakespeare's mind and manners brightly shines
    In his well-turned, and true-filed lines;
In each of which he seems to shake a lance,
    As brandish'd at the eyes of ignorance.
Sweet Swan of Avon! what a sight it were
    To see thee in our waters yet appear,
And make those flights upon the banks of Thames,
    That so did take Eliza and our James!
But stay, I see thee in the hemisphere
    Advanc'd, and made a constellation there!
Shine forth, thou star of poets, and with rage
    Or influence, chide or cheer the drooping stage...

"Sweet Swan of Avon" indeed! It cannot reasonably be doubted that Jonson was as fully in the picture on the matter of the
authorship as we now are. In his time, nothing could have been
more obvious than that the scarcely-known-of Shakespeare was
not, and could not have been, the author of some of the most
powerful and impressive literature ever written in any language.
In any case, fully involved in the publishing of the First Folio as
he was, he was clearly a party to the falsifying of the authorship.

Ben Jonson, incidentally, was himself a notable playwright of
that period. Although, by contrast with the various supposed authors of that time whom we have glanced at briefly, I know of no
reason to suppose that he was one of Bacon's masks, I do think it
highly probable, if only because of the "Shakespearean" richness
and general style of the composition, that both of the pieces of
verse quoted above were written by Bacon, who has given us

good reason to suppose that modesty was not one of his virtues. Be that as it may or may not be: either way Bacon must have had a close enough relationship with Jonson to persuade him to become as fully involved with the First Folio as we have seen him to be and, no less remarkable, to put his name to such an extraordinary piece of verse about a rival playwright and thus allow himself to be so prominently included as a selling-point for this First Folio.

*   *   *   *   *

Enough of Jonson. It is time for us to pursue one last mystery connected with the William Shaksper commonly reckoned to be William Shakespeare: what he actually *looked* like.

Over the centuries several pictures have been found, some of them even only quite recently, on behalf of which it has been claimed that they are authentic portraits of the William Shakespeare of Stratford. I am now giving a sample of them together with (a) the dates on which they were identified as possibilities and (b) such facts and generally-held opinions about them as I am aware of. I am saving until last the one that is generally rated as most probable by most expert Stratfordians – "Stratfordian" being a commonly-used label for those who hold that Stratford's William Shaksper was William Shakespeare – and that I referred to on page 153 and elsewhere.

The portrait on the next page, known as the Chandos portrait is dated in the early 1600s and attributed to the contemporary artist John Taylor, although this is not considered as capable of proof and therefore as definite.

Taylor was a prominent member, of the Worshipful Company of Painter-Stainers, an organisation based in the City of London that still exists for the purpose of promoting fine arts and decorative arts; and the company's collection of portraits included one of him. He ended up in the senor position of Master in that organisation.

The Chandos portrait.

The portrait is named after the Duke of Chandos, who once owned the painting. It has been described as featuring a gypsy-like poet with a gold earring in his left ear, a long moustache, short beard, long, messy hair, an open collar. It was given to the National Portrait Gallery in London on its foundation in 1856 and is listed as the first work in its collection.

The Cobbe portrait, on this page, is an early Jacobean panel-painting of a gentleman that has been argued to be a life portrait of William Shakespeare

The Cobbe portrait.

It was only identified in 2006, and until then had been completely unknown to the world. It has been the centre-piece of two exhibitions dedicated to it: *Shakespeare Found: a Life Portrait* at the Shakespeare Birthplace Trust, Stratford-upon-Avon, from April–October 2009, and *The Changing Face of William Shakespeare* at the Morgan Library and Museum, New York, from February–May 2011.

Of the Janssen portrait, there are two versions, the first of which, chronologically, is on this page. This version is prior to one before a restoration that was made in 1988. The version after that restoration is on the next page.

The Janssen portrait

before its restoration in 1988.

This second other version of the Janssen portrait, is the portrait after an "over-painting" done in the 18th century was removed. The reason for the original "over-painting" is thought to have been to make the portrait to look more like Shakespeare.

The Janssen portrait

after its restoration in 1988.

The portrait on the next page, the Sanders portrait, is reputed to be one of the only images of William Shakespeare belonging to his lifetime. It features a middle-aged man wearing a black doublet with silver ornamentation.

The Sanders portrait.

It also has a label affixed to the back which reads:

Shakespere
Born April 23-1564
Died April 23-1616
Aged 52
This Likeness taken 1603
Age at that time 39 y^s

That label was transcribed in 1909 by Marion Henry Spielmann. Today, the original text on the portrait is not legible.

The Grafton portrait is by an unknown artist. The date, 1588, is just visible at the top right-hand corner, and the painting is indeed believed to date back to Shakespeare's lifetime. The claim that it is a painting intended to represent him is considered to be discredited.

The Grafton portrait.

Finally...!

On the next two pages will be found two representations of the famous, and even iconic, engraving that, as already noted, features as the frontispiece for the title page of the 1623 First Folio. It is the portrait known as the Martin Droeshout portrait, and is thus-called on the supposition, supported by the words at the bottom of the actual portrait, that it was engraved by an English engraver of that name, of Flemish descent. Because of its unique significance, I am giving (a) two versions of it, both intended to represent the same engraving, and (b) in addition, an enlarged portion of the first of the two versions, that shows more detail.

Below is the engraving that is the **Droeshout portrait,** dated 1622, as written on the portrait.

On the next page is...

Another depiction of the Droeshout engraving, showing more detail

The Droeshout portrait is generally reckoned to be the most accurate representation of the appearance of Shakespeare, and indeed to be a reasonably close likeness. The main support for that view comes from Ben Jonson, who indicated that that was his view. Here is the part of his ten-line poem quoted earlier that is relevant to that:

> This Figure that thou here seest put,
> It was for gentle Shakespeare cut,
> Wherein the Graver had a strife
> With Nature, to out-doo the life:
> O, could he have but drawn his wit
> As well in brasse, as he has hit
> His face...

Let us now consider the Droeshout portrait with appropriate care, to see if I was justified in describing it, back on page 198, as "very, very strange".

Here are some features of it that surely fit it into that category.

– The head is not positioned so as to be able to belong physically to the body. It is too high above the shoulders – no neck could be as long as that. Its physical relationship to the rest of the body, starting with the shoulders, is as no head of any man or woman could be.

– The head is disproportionately large in relation to body. It is the same height from the top of the forehead to the chin as the body is from the bottom of the head to its waist. Normal would be for the head to be about half the size of that part of the body.

– The nose is out of alignment. The middle of the upper lip is not where it ought to be, but is clearly under the left nostril.

– There is stubble on the face, almost immediately under the lower lip and definitely prominent, indicative that the face portrayed has not having shaved for about two days. Scruffy would fairly describe that aspect of the face, which of course would be unimaginable in any sort of normal representation of someone that was intended to be used as an official portrait.

– The *left*-hand corner of the collar (that is to say, the corner on the right of the picture) is a different shape, that of a ninety-degree corner of a rectangle, from the shape of the *right*-hand corner (the corner on the left of the picture), which is less than ninety degrees.

– The right-hand shoulder of the person portrayed, the shoulder on the left of the picture, does not have the appearance of a right-hand shoulder. As you can see if you look at it carefully, and indeed as a professional tailor has publicly confirmed (in an article in *Gentleman's Tailor Magazine*, April 1911), what is depicted is in fact as though it was the left-hand

209

shoulder *viewed from the back*. In other words, both shoulders in the supposed portrait are clearly left-hand shoulders.

– The pattern of the garment on the left-hand shoulder is noticeably different from the pattern on the right-hand shoulder.

– Indeed there is a line along the part of the face running from just where hair ends on the face's left side to about halfway to the bottom of the chin, which clearly indicates a mask.

All the anomalies pointed out so far are, in my submission, obvious as soon as attention is drawn to them. The one that I am coming to now, which will conclude what I am drawing attention to under the heading of the Droeshout portrait, is more subtle but still can be seen to be definite once it is examined with reasonable care. It was brought to my notice on page 36 of an interesting book published in 1951, *The Shaksper Illusion* by Edward D. Johnson.

If you look carefully at the eyes, you will see that they are definitely abnormal, in that they are simply not a normal right eye and left eye. Rather, they are *both* of them right eyes.

There is no need for us to rely solely on the word of Edward Johnson for that judgement. On the same page 36, he quotes a Harley Street oculist (eye specialist), Dr. W. Russell Brain, to the following effect. If you examine the left eye in the picture, you will see that the half of the upper eyelid nearest to the nose is four times the width of the half of the upper lid furthest from the nose. Thus what should be the left eye is in fact another right eye. This, Johnson says, becomes obvious if one covers up the right eye, the nose and the mouth.

Clearly the face is a mask, identifiably so: a mask that is real and visible in the engraving.

*   *   *   *   *

The mystery that is involved in that picture must surely be a signal that there is a mystery involved in everything to do with

Shakespeare. On a subject of genuinely great interest, as of course is the case with almost anything to do with Shakespeare, there could be no purpose in creating any such a mystery that was attached *only* to a picture.

The reality that a mystery of that nature must embrace not only the picture that we have been examining, but everything connected to it; and that of course means that, again as with everything to do with Shakespeare, it is a mystery that is sinister and creepy.

Might I be accused, in saying that, of suddenly wading into the realms of exaggeration and unreasonableness? If I were so accused, I would most forcefully deny that charge. Please, gracious reader, do not forget the play *Macb*th*.

Yes, *everything* to do with Shakespeare is, in my submission, a combination of one gigantic – and sinister and creepy – mystery: a mystery to which, in all the foregoing, I have offered what appears to be, beyond any doubt, its *only* possible solution, and one that, *in its totality*, has to the best of my knowledge never appeared in print before.

*   *   *   *   *

As to what the author of the works of Shakespeare *really* looked like, this we can certainly know.

When Francis Bacon died in 1626 he was buried in St. Michael's Church in Saint Albans in the county of Hertfordshire, which was near to where he lived, in Gorhambury.

It is on record that shortly after his burial, a friend of his who had acted as his secretary, Sir Thomas Meauty, organised and paid for a memorial in the form of a large statue showing Bacon seated, with his left elbow resting on the arm of a chair and his, with his right hand supporting the right side his head.

Here are two photographs of the statue, which, as well as the statue, can still be viewed today in St Michael's Church.

At the base of the statue is carved, in Latin script, the following (now translated into English):

Francis Bacon
Baron of Verulam, Viscount of St. Albans
or, by more conspicuous titles
of Science the Light, of Eloquence the Law, sat thus.
Who after all Natural Wisdom
And Secret of Civil Life he had unfolded,
Nature's life fulfilled -
Let Compounds be
Dissolved!
In the year of our Lord 1626, aged 66.

It need hardly be said that it is in very many ways a grossly inappropriate depiction of a dead person for placement inside a church, and I do not suppose there is anything else like it in any traditional church building anywhere in the world.

With Francis Bacon, absolutely *nothing* is *ever* right; not even the way in which he features in a statue of him in a church. He can, surely, be fairly described as both a genius and a creepy piece of human vermin.

*   *   *   *   *

I bring this chapter, and this book, to an end by quoting the final sentence of a book that, were it not for the book by Sir Sidney Lee (*A Life of William Shakespeare*) referred to back in chapter 6 of PART II, could be in my opinion – in the words I used there – "a strong candidate for the title, the most remarkable book ever written".

By contrast with the 766 pages of Sir Sidney's book, this one, *Shakespeare The Biography* by the well-regarded author Peter Ackroyd published in 2005 (Chatto & Windus, London), occupies a "mere" 566 pages. Even that, however, is remarkable given that, as we have seen, the *known* biographical details of William Shakespeare are not sufficient to fill up *a single page* of any ordinary book, which meant that those biographical details needed to be supplemented by the "might be's", "could have been's", "it can be supposed's" and so on, as indeed they are, in profusion, in Mr. Ackroyd's book. (Not least remarkable is that nowhere in his book, not even when referring to other members of the Shaksper family, does Mr. Ackroyd's spell the name of its subject other than as "Shakespeare" – which of course no member of the Stratfordian family ever did.)

Anyway, surely worth reproducing here, for the entertainment of my readers, is the sentence with which Mr. Ackroyd concludes his book in its very last chapter. Referring to the 1623 First Folio, he says there:

The volume is adorned by the Droeshout engraving of the dramatist [see pages 164 and 165 above], which is indeed the only generally accepted likeness of William Shakespeare.

Yes, Mr. Ackroyd really did say "generally accepted likeness"! And he uses those words, "generally accepted",

...even though the so-called *likeness* is in fact a clearly visible *mask*

˙...and even though *both* of the mask's eyes are right eyes, rather than one left eye and one right eye

...and even though the head and the body are grotesquely out of proportion to each other in terms of size

...and so on, and so on...

Readers may be tempted to wonder if Mr. Ackroyd was being facetious. But no, I have re-read the book's closing paragraph that ended with that sentence, and he clearly wrote those words in all seriousness. Furthermore, because of his status as a respected author, I think we can safely assume that he knows what he is talking about when he uses the term "generally accepted".

From that it follows that, in a single sentence – when taken in the context of what we have been looking at as to (a) the *reality* of William Shakespeare, and (b), in particular, the devastatingly *obvious* impossibility that the 1623 First Folio's "William Shakespeare" could be the illiterate Stratfordian, Will Shaksper – Mr. Ackroyd has taught us all that we need to know about present-day academia in the world of literature.

Against that background, at least some of my readers can breathe a sigh of contentment. Indeed to those of you who have run away from Shakespeare or have read him or watched him only because you thought you ought to, I say: Congratulations! Far from you having been at fault, it is *you*, and not the worshippers of Shakespeare, who have got it right!

APPENDIX
Other notable critics of William Shakespeare

Because of what I am about to quote, and because, too, of where and how it fits in with the rest of this book, I believe that I have good reason to believe this appendix to be considerably more important than are the great majority of appendices in books. It is worth my explaining why.

In what I have said in Part I of this book, where I addressed what I claim to be the too-little-recognised *reality* of Shakespeare, I consider myself to have been subject to considerable limitations in what I could justifiably say to his discredit, even though that leaves that part of the subject Shakespeare rather incomplete.

The reason for these limitations is that, as a matter of policy, I needed to limit myself strictly to presenting undoubted facts that are either obvious or adequately documented, such as – to give just one example – the amount of violence that most of Shakespeare's plays are so extraordinarily full of. It would have been pointless, and even potentially damaging to how convincingly I could present my case, if I had *also* included personal judgements given by me – however reasonable they might be – of the quality of Shakespeare's play-writing, in respect of his competence (a) in the construction of the plays, (b) in his delineation of the characters in the plays, and (c) in what is said by the characters in the plays and how they say whatever it is that they say.

By contrast with the features of Shakespeare that I did address, whatever I might choose to say on the matters just mentioned in (a), (b) and (c) above could only represent *my own considered judgement and opinion* on such matters. If I might think something to be discreditable, I would not, by the very nature of such things, be able to support whatever I said with anything resembling objective and inescapable proof.

Any unsupported judgements and opinions given by me on any matter in this book would, in their effects, simply amount to inviting the countless people who can be expected to be hostile to my position on Shakespeare to denounce me as hopelessly incompetent when making such judgements and giving such opinions. Indeed critics could maintain that whatever I said under these headings was *in itself* sufficient proof of my incompetence in relation to the whole subject of Shakespeare. What is more, there would be nothing compelling that I could say in response: it would be simply a matter of my judgement versus theirs, with the word "theirs" covering all the most highly regarded Shakespeare scholars living and dead.

Against that background, I now remind readers that, in this book's Preface, I said that I thought that I could justifiably believe my offering on William Shakespeare to be – the highlighting is now being added by me – "...one of *very few* books ever published to take its particular position on the first of its two main topics" – that first topic being the quality of its content, the influence of which, again in my words, "has almost certainly been greater by far than the influence exercised by any other single person during those centuries, not excluding the best-known politicians and philosophers of the era."

The words "one of *very few* books ever published" in that sentence made it clear, of course, that what I was *not* claiming was to be *completely alone* in my position. Nor indeed am I completely alone. Furthermore, critics who are in a certain amount of agreement with my general position include some prominent and highly regarded authors, perhaps the most noteworthy of which are Russia's most widely admired author Count Leo Nikolayevich Tolstoy, and Mr. George Bernard Shaw, Voltaire (M. François-Marie Arouet) and Mr. J. R. R. Tolkien.

Of those, the one who took the subject most seriously was Count Tolstoy, who put his thoughts together in a short book (104 pages) that has been published in English under the title *Tolstoy on Shakespeare – A Critical Essay on Shakespeare*. I am now quoting some extracts from that book that appear to me particularly significant and revealing. Those who wish to read the book in full will find that it is readily available.

Mr. Crosby's article "Shakespeare's attitude toward the working classes" suggested to me the idea of also expressing my own long-established opinion about the works of Shakespeare, in direct opposition, as it is, to that established in all the whole European world. Calling to mind all the struggle of doubt and self-deceit – in my efforts to attune myself to Shakespeare – which I went through owing to my complete disagreement with this universal adulation, and, presuming that many have experienced and are experiencing the same, I think that it may not be unprofitable to express definitely and frankly this view of mine, opposed to that of the majority. Indeed all the more does this seem appropriate given the conclusions to which I came when examining the causes of my disagreement with the universally established opinion, and which are, it seems to me, not without interest and significance.

I remember the astonishment I felt when I first read Shakespeare. I expected to receive a powerful aesthetic pleasure, but having read, one after the other, works regarded as his best: *King Lear, Romeo and Juliet, Hamlet* and *Macbeth*, not only did I feel no delight, but I felt an irresistible repulsion and tedium, and wondered whether I was senseless in feeling works regarded as the summit of perfection by the whole of the civilized world to be trivial and positively bad, or whether the significance which this civilised world attributes to the works of Shakespeare was itself senseless.

My consternation was increased by the fact that I have always keenly felt the beauties of poetry in every form. I wondered why artistic works recognized by the whole world as those of a genius – the works of Shakespeare – should not only *fail to please me*, but *be actually disagreeable to me*?

For a long time I could not believe in myself, and during fifty years, in order to test myself, I several times recommenced reading Shakespeare in every possible form, in Russian, in English and in German, as I was advised. I read the dramas and the comedies and historical plays several times, and invariably underwent the same feelings: repulsion, weariness, and bewilderment.

At the present time, before writing this preface, being desirous once more to test myself, I have, as an old man of seventy-five, again read the whole of Shakespeare, including the historical plays, the *Henrys*, *Troilus and Cressida*, *The Tempest*, *Cymbeline*. Rather, I have felt, with even greater force, the same feelings – but this time not of bewilderment but of firm, indubitable conviction that the unquestionable glory of a great genius which Shakespeare enjoys, and which compels writers of our time to imitate him and readers and spectators to discover in him non-existent merits – thereby distorting their aesthetic and ethical understanding – is a great evil, as is every untruth.

Although I know that the majority of people so firmly believe in the greatness of Shakespeare that, in reading this judgment of mine, they will not admit even the *possibility* of its justice, and will not give it the slightest attention, nevertheless I will endeavour, as well as I can, to show why I believe that Shakespeare cannot be recognized either as a great genius, or even as an *average* author.

For illustration of my purpose I will take one of Shakespeare's most extolled dramas, *King Lear*, in the enthusiastic praise of which the majority of critics agree...

After trumpets are blown, King Lear enters with his daughters and sons-in-law, and utters a speech to the effect that, owing to old age, he wishes to retire from the cares of business and divide his kingdom between his daughters. In order to know how much he should give to each daughter, he announces that, to the one who says she loves him most, he will give most.

The eldest daughter, Goneril, says that words cannot express the extent of her love; that she loves her father more than eyesight, space, and liberty; that she loves him so much that it "makes her breath poor". King Lear immediately allots his daughter, on the map, her portion of fields, woods, rivers, and meadows, and then asks the same question of the second daughter.

The second daughter, Regan, says that her sister has correctly expressed her own feelings, but not strongly enough. She, Regan, loves her father so much that everything is abhorrent to her except his love.

The king rewards this daughter also. He then asks his youngest, the favourite, in whom, according to his expression, are "interess'd the vines of France and the milk of Burgundy," that is, whose hand is being claimed by the King of France and the Duke of Burgundy. He asks Cordelia how she loves him.

Cordelia, who personifies all the virtues, as the eldest two personify all the vices, says, quite out of place, as if on purpose to irritate her father, that, although she loves and honours him and is grateful to him, yet if she marries, the entirety of her love will not belong to her father, but she will also love her husband.

Hearing these words, the King loses his temper, and curses this favourite daughter with the most dreadful and strange maledictions, saying, for instance, that he will henceforth love his daughter as little as he loves the man who devours his own children...

Not to mention the pompous, characterless language of King Lear, the same in which all Shakespeare's Kings speak, the reader, or spectator, cannot conceive that a King, however old and stupid he may be, could believe the words of the vicious daughters, with whom he had passed his whole life, and *not* believe his favourite daughter, but, on the contrary, would curse and banish her. The spectator or reader, therefore, cannot share the feelings of the persons participating in this unnatural scene...

In this celebrated drama, however absurd it may appear in my rendering (which I have endeavoured to make as impartial as possible), I may confidently say that, in the original, it is *even more* absurd. For any man of our time – if he were not under the hypnotic suggestion that this drama is the height of perfection – it would be enough to read it to its end (if he were to have sufficient patience for this) to be convinced that, *far* from being the height of perfection, it is a very bad, carelessly composed production, which, even if it could have been of interest to a certain public at a certain time, cannot evoke among us anything but aversion and weariness.

Every reader of our time who is free from the influence of suggestion will also receive exactly the same impression from all the other extolled dramas of Shakespeare, not to mention the senseless, dramatized tales, *Pericles, Twelfth Night, The Tempest, Cymbeline, Troilus and Cressida.*

Unfortunately, however, such free-minded individuals, not inoculated with Shakespeare-worship, are no longer to be found in our Christian society. Every man of our society and time, from the first period of his conscious life, has been inoculated with the idea that Shakespeare is a genius, a poet, and a dramatist, and that all his writings are the height of perfection...

Dramatic art, according to the laws established by those very critics who extol Shakespeare, demands that the persons represented in the play should be, in consequence of actions proper to their characters, and owing to a natural course of events, placed in positions requiring them to struggle with the surrounding world to which they find themselves in opposition, and that in this struggle they should display their inherent qualities.

In *King Lear* the persons represented are indeed placed externally in opposition to the outward world; and they do indeed struggle with it. But their strife does not flow from the natural course of events nor from their own characters. It is quite *arbitrarily* established by the author, and it therefore cannot produce on the reader the illusion which represents the essential condition of art.

Lear has no necessity or motive for his abdication. Also, having lived all his life with his daughters, he has no reason to believe the words of the two elders and not the truthful

220

statement of the youngest. Yet *upon that* the whole tragedy of his position is built.

This is in the first place.

Secondly, in this, as in the other dramas of Shakespeare, all the characters live, think, speak and act quite unconformably with the given time and place. The action of *King Lear* takes place 800 years B.C., and yet the characters are placed in conditions possible only in the Middle Ages. Participating in the drama are kings, dukes, armies, and illegitimate children, and gentlemen, courtiers, doctors, farmers, officers, soldiers, and knights with vizors, etc.

It is possible that such anachronisms (with which Shakespeare's dramas abound) did not injure the possibility of illusion in the sixteenth century and the beginning of the seventeenth. In our time, however, it is no longer possible to follow with interest the development of events which one knows could not take place in the conditions which the author describes in detail. The artificiality of the positions, not flowing from the natural course of events, or from the nature of the characters and their want of conformity with time and space, is further increased by those coarse embellishments which are continually added by Shakespeare and intended to appear particularly touching. The extraordinary storm during which King Lear roams about the heath, or the grass which for some reason he puts on his head – as does Ophelia in *Hamlet* – or Edgar's attire, or the fool's speeches, or the appearance of the helmeted horseman, Edgar: all these effects not only fail to enhance the impression, *but produce an opposite effect*. It often happens that even during these obviously intentional efforts after effect, as, for instance, the dragging out by the legs of half a dozen corpses, with which all Shakespeare's tragedies terminate, instead of feeling fear and pity, one is tempted rather to laugh...

But it is not enough that Shakespeare's characters are placed in tragic positions which are impossible, do not flow from the course of events, and are inappropriate to time and space. These personages, besides this, act in a way which is out of keeping with their definite character, and is quite arbitrary. It is generally asserted that in Shakespeare's dramas the characters are especially well expressed; that, notwithstanding their vividness, they are many-sided, like those of living people; that, while exhibiting the characteristics of a given individual, they at the same time wear the features of man in general. It is usual to say that the delineation of character in Shakespeare is the height of perfection.

This is asserted with such confidence and repeated by all as indisputable truth; but, however much I endeavoured to find confirmation of this in Shakespeare's dramas, I always found the opposite. In reading any of Shakespeare's dramas whatever, I was, from the very first, instantly convinced that he was lacking in the most important, if not the only, means of portraying characters. That is to say, individuality of language, *i.e.*, the style of speech of every person being natural to his character, is absent from Shakespeare. All his characters speak, not their own, but always one and the same Shakespearian, pretentious and unnatural language, in which not only they could not speak, but in which no living man has *ever* spoken or does speak...

Thus it is in the drama we are examining, which Shakespeare has borrowed from the drama *King Lear*. Thus it is also with *Othello*, taken from an Italian romance, and with the famous *Hamlet*. The same with Antony, Brutus, Cleopatra, Shylock, Richard, and all Shakespeare's characters, that are all taken from some antecedent work. Shakespeare, while profiting by characters already given in preceding dramas, or romances, chronicles, or Plutarch's *Lives*, not only fails to render them more truthful and vivid, notwithstanding his eulogists assert, but, on the contrary, always weakens them and often completely destroys them, as with Lear, compelling his characters to commit actions unnatural to them, and, above all, to utter speeches natural neither to them nor to any one whatever...

Shakespeare's characters continually do and say what is not only *unnatural* to them, but utterly *unnecessary*. I do not cite examples of this, because I believe that he who does not himself see this striking deficiency in all Shakespeare's dramas will not be persuaded by any examples and proofs. It is sufficient to read *King Lear* alone, with its insanity, murders, plucking out of eyes, Gloucester's jump, its poisonings, and wranglings – not to mention *Pericles*, *Cymbeline*, *The Winter's Tale*, *The Tempest* – to be convinced of this. *Only a man devoid of the sense of measure and of taste could produce such types as Titus Andronicus or Troilus and Cressida...*

The merit of every poetic work depends on three things:

(1) The subject of the work: the deeper the subject, *i.e.*, the more important it is to the life of mankind, the higher is the work.

(2) The external beauty achieved by technical methods proper to the particular kind of art. Thus, in dramatic art, the technical method will be a true individuality of language, corresponding to the characters; a natural, and at the same time touching plot; a correct scenic rendering of the demonstration and development of emotion; and the feeling of measure in all that is represented.

(3) Sincerity, *i.e.*, that the author should himself keenly feel what he expresses. Without this condition there can be no work of art, as the essence of art consists in the contemplation of the work of art being infected with the author's feeling. If the author does not actually feel what he expresses, then the recipient cannot become infected with the feeling of the author, and does not experience any feeling; and the production can no longer be classified as a work of art.

The subject of Shakespeare's pieces, as is seen from the demonstrations of his greatest admirers, is the lowest, most vulgar view of life, which regards the external elevation of the lords of the world as a genuine distinction, despises the crowd, *i.e.*, the working classes – repudiates not only all religious strivings directed to the betterment of the existing order, but also all humanitarian strivings so directed.

The second condition also, with the exception of the rendering of the scenes in which the movement of feelings is expressed, is quite absent in Shakespeare. He does not grasp the natural character of the positions of his personages, nor the language of the persons represented, nor the feeling of measure without which no work can be artistic.

The third and most important condition, sincerity, is completely absent in all Shakespeare's works. In all of them one sees intentional artifice; one sees that he is not *in earnest*, but that he is playing with words...

Many times during my life I have had occasion to argue about Shakespeare with his admirers, not only with people little sensitive to poetry but with those who keenly felt poetic beauty; and every time I encountered one and the same attitude toward my objection to the praises of Shakespeare. I was not refuted when I pointed out Shakespeare's defects; they only offered me condolences for my want of comprehension, and urged upon me the necessity of recognising the extraordinary supernatural grandeur of Shakespeare. And they did not explain to me in what the beauties of Shakespeare consisted, but were merely vaguely and exaggeratedly enraptured with the whole of Shakespeare, extolling some favourite passages: the unbuttoning of Lear's button, Falstaff's lying, Lady Macbeth's ineffaceable spots, Hamlet's exhortation to his father's ghost, "forty thousand brothers," etc.

"Open Shakespeare wherever you like," I used to say to these admirers, "or wherever it may chance, and you will see that you will never find ten consecutive lines which are comprehensible, unartificial, natural to the character that says them, and which produce an artistic impression." (This experiment may be made by anyone. And either at random, or according to their own choice.) Shakespeare's admirers opened pages in Shakespeare's dramas, and, without paying any attention to my criticisms as to why the selected ten lines did not satisfy the most elementary demands of aesthetic and common sense, they were enchanted with the very thing that to me appeared absurd, incomprehensible, and inartistic...

Until the end of the eighteenth century Shakespeare not only failed to gain any special fame in England, but was valued less than his contemporary dramatists: Ben Jonson, Fletcher, Beaumont, and others. His fame originated in Germany, and thence was transferred to England...

Because of the clever development of scenes which constituted Shakespeare's peculiarity, they chose Shakespeare's dramas in preference to all other English dramas, and excluded those which were not in the least inferior, but were even superior, to Shakespeare. At the head of the group stood Goethe, who was then the dictator of public opinion in aesthetic questions. He it was who, partly owing to a desire to destroy the fascination of the false French art, partly owing to his desire to give a greater scope to his own dramatic writing, but chiefly through the agreement of his view of life with Shakespeare's, declared Shakespeare a great poet.

When this error was announced by an authority like Goethe, all those aesthetic critics who did not understand art threw themselves on it like crows on carrion and began to discover in Shakespeare beauties which did not exist, and to extol them. These men – German aesthetic critics, for the most part utterly devoid of aesthetic feeling, without that simple, direct artistic sensibility which, for people with a feeling for art, clearly distinguishes aesthetic impressions from all others, but believing the authority which had recognized Shakespeare as a great poet – began to praise the whole of Shakespeare indiscriminately, especially distinguishing such passages as struck them by their effects, or which expressed thoughts corresponding to their views of life, imagining that these effects and these thoughts constitute the essence of what is called art. These men acted as blind men would act who endeavoured to find diamonds by touch among a heap of stones they were fingering. As the blind man would for a long time strenuously handle the stones and in the end would come to no other conclusion than that all stones are precious and especially so the smoothest, so also these aesthetic critics, without artistic feeling, could not but come to similar results in relation to Shakespeare...

It is these people who are chiefly responsible for Shakespeare's fame. It was principally owing to their writings that the interaction took place between writers and public which expressed itself, and is still expressing itself, in an insane worship of Shakespeare which has no rational foundation. These aesthetic critics have written profound treatises about Shakespeare. Eleven thousand volumes have been written about him, and a whole science of Shakespeareology composed; while the public, on the one hand, took more and more interest, and the learned critics, on the other hand, gave further and further explanations, adding to the confusion...

At the beginning of the last century, when Goethe was dictator of philosophic thought and aesthetic laws, a series of casual circumstances made him praise Shakespeare. The aesthetic critics caught up this praise and took to writing their lengthy, misty, learned articles, and the great European public began to be enchanted with Shakespeare. The critics, answering to the popular interest, and endeavouring to compete with one another, wrote new essays about Shakespeare; the readers and spectators on their side were increasingly confirmed in their admiration, and Shakespeare's fame, like a lump of snow, kept growing and growing, until in our time it has attained that insane worship which obviously has no other foundation than "suggestion".

Shakespeare finds no rival, not even approximately, either among the old or the new writers. Here are some of the tributes paid to him.

"Poetic truth is the brightest flower in the crown of Shakespeare's merits."

"Shakespeare is the greatest moralist of all times."

"Shakespeare exhibits such many-sidedness and such objectivism that they carry him beyond the limits of time and nationality."

"Shakespeare is the greatest genius that has hitherto existed."

"For the creation of tragedy, comedy, history, idyll, idyllistic comedy, aesthetic idyll, for the profoundest presentation, or for any casually thrown off, passing piece of verse, he is the only man. He not only wields an unlimited power over our mirth and our tears, over all the workings of passion, humour, thought, and observation, but he possesses also an infinite region full of the phantasy of fiction, of a horrifying and an amusing character. He possesses penetration both in the world of fiction and of reality, and above this reigns one and the same truthfulness to character and to nature, and the same spirit of humanity."

"To Shakespeare the epithet of Great comes of itself; and if one adds that independently of his greatness he has, further, become the reformer of all literature, and, moreover, has in his works not only expressed the phenomenon of life as it was in his day, but also, by the genius of thought which floated in the air has prophetically forestalled the direction that the social spirit was going to take in the future (of which we see a striking example in *Hamlet*) – one may, without hesitation, say that Shakespeare was not only a great poet, but the greatest of all poets who ever existed, and that in the sphere of poetic creation his only worthy rival was that same life which in his works he expressed to such perfection."

The obvious exaggeration of this estimate proves more conclusively than anything that it is the consequence, not of common sense, but of suggestion. The more trivial, the lower, the emptier a phenomenon is, if only it has become the subject of suggestion, the more supernatural and exaggerated is the significance attributed to it...

Another deplorable result of this worship is the presentation to men of a false model for imitation. If people wrote of Shakespeare that for his time he was a good writer, that he had a fairly good turn for verse, was an intelligent actor and good stage-manager – even were this appreciation incorrect and somewhat exaggerated – if only it were moderately true, people of the rising generation might remain free from Shakespeare's influence. But when every young man entering into life in our time has presented to him, as the model of moral perfection, not the religious and moral teachers of mankind, but first of all Shakespeare, concerning whom it has been decided and is handed down by learned men from generation to generation, as an incontestable truth, that he was the greatest poet, the greatest teacher of life, the young man cannot remain free from this pernicious influence. When he is reading or listening to Shakespeare the question for him is no longer whether Shakespeare be good or bad, but only: In what consists that extraordinary beauty, both aesthetic and ethical, of which he has been assured by learned men whom he respects, and which he himself neither sees nor feels? And constraining himself, and distorting his aesthetic and ethical feeling, he tries to conform to the ruling opinion. He no longer believes in himself, but in what is said by the learned people whom he respects.

BIBLIOGRAPHY

The output of literature on matters concerning Shakespeare is of course vast, as indeed even the output of literature on matters concerning Shakespeare and of works addressing the authorship, whether solely or as part of a wider treatment of the Shakespeare subject.

On the other hand, the number of published writings, whether books, booklets, pamphlets or articles in periodical articles, that address the topic that PART I in particular is concerned with is minuscule. Certainly, notwithstanding reasonably diligent searching over a period of many years, I have never found any, other than the five mentioned in the Appendix.

Against that background, I am mainly – though not entirely – limiting myself to naming the books-and-authors that I made reference to in the foregoing text. Inclusion of a book or booklet in the lists below does not necessarily imply that I consider it to be sound, even in part, let alone in its entirely. Occasionally, after all, I have quoted something in order to disagree with it.

Books on or relevant to Shakespeare which make no reference, even by implication, to Francis Bacon or any other possible author or authors.

Ackroyd, Peter. *Shakespeare – The Biography*. Chatto & Windus, London, 2005

Benedictine Abbey of Croyland. *The Croyland Chronicle*.

Chambers, E. K. *William Shakespeare. A Study of Facts and Problems*. Clarendon Press, Oxford, 1930

Chauvette, Charlotte. Magazine article titled "Defining Early Modern Pornography: The Case of Venus and Adonis" in Winter 2012 edition (volume 12, number 1) of *The Journal for Early Modern Cultural Studies*. University of Pennsylvania Press.

Collins, Professor Churton. *Studies in Shakespeare*. Archibald Constable & Co, London, 1904.

Croyland Chronicle, The. A historical record compiled by the Benedictine Abbey of Croyland, in Lincolnshire.

Edwards, William Henry. *Shaksper Not Shakespeare*. The Robert Clarke Company, Cincinnati, 1900.

Huggett, Richard. *The Curse of Macbeth and Other Theatrical Superstitions*. Picton Publishing, Chippenham, 1981.

Jenkins, Simon. *A Short History of England*. Profile Books, 2011.

Johnson, Edward D. *The Shaksper Illusion*. George Lapworth & Co., London, 1951.

Lee, Sir Sidney. *A Life of William Shakespeare*. Macmillan, 1898.

More, Saint-and-Sir Thomas (attributed to). *The History of King Richard III*.

Owen Dr. Orville. *Sir Francis Bacon's Cipher Story* (originally in five volumes). 1893-1985. A volume currently in print: Andesite Press, 2015. N.B. What Dr. Owen's five-volume compilation is "all about" is conveniently summarised in a collection of articles "Shakespeare-Bacon in a periodical, the *Detroit Journal* (of Detroit, Michigan), articles titled by George P. Goodale, the dramatic critic of the *Detroit Journal*, which appeared in the *Detroit Journal* of 14th September 1893.

Oxford University Press. *Oxford Dictionary of National Biography*. 1882, and with supplements continually added until 1990.

Pointon, A. J. *The Man Who Was Never Shakespeare*. Parapress, Tunbridge Wells, 2011.

Schoenbaum, Professor S. *William Shakespeare – a Documentary Life*. Clarendon Press, Oxford, 1975.

Shakespeare, William (attributed to).

Sokol, Professor B. J. and Dr. Mary (joint-authors). *Shakespeare's Legal Language – A Dictionary*. Athlone Press, London and New York, 2000 and 2004.

Sydenham of Combe, Lord, and H. C. Crouch. *The "Shakespeare" Myth: A Challenge.* (Booklet, 30 pages. Cornwall Press, England, 1924.

Books taking the position that the author of the works of Willian Shakespeare must have been written by someone else, such as Sir Francis Bacon.

Altrocchi, Paul Hemenway, M.D. *Avalanche of Falsity: Volume 7: Fraudulent Misinformation Highlights the Case for Shakspere of Stratford.* Universe, Indiana, 2014.

Campbell, the Right Honourable Lord (John). *Shakespeare's Legal Acquirements Considered.* D. Appleton and Co., 1859.

Fellows, Virginia M. *The Shakespeare Code.* 1st Books Library, 2000.

Fuller, Jean Overton. *Sir Francis Bacon – A Biography.* East West Publications 1981; revised edition George Mann of Maidstone, 1994.

Goodale, George P. Article "Shakespeare-Bacon" in *Detroit Journal*, 14th September 1893.

Greenwood, G. G. *The Shakespeare Problem Restated.* John Lane and Bodley Head, London, 1907.

Greenwood, G. G., Elsie Greenwood and Lord Ponsonby of Shulbrede. *The Shakespeare Problem Restated.* Athenaeum Press, London, 1937.

Holmes, Nathaniel. *The Authorship of Shakespeare* (two volumes). Houghton, Miffles and Company, Boston and New York, 1887.

Marche, Stephen. *How Shakespeare Changed Everything.* Harper Perennial, New York, 2011.

Theobald, Bertram G., B.A. *Francis Bacon Concealed and Revealed.* Cecil Palmer, London, 1930.

Woodward, Parker. *Tudor Problems.* Gay and Hancock, London, 1912.

Books that are not specifically related to Shakespeare but are of some relevance.

Glenn, Msgr. Paul J. *An Introduction to Philosophy.* Herder Book Co., St. Luis, U.S.A., 1944.

Weir, Alison. *Elizabeth the Queen.* Vintage Books, New York, 2009.

Tombs, Robert. *The English and Their History.* Penguin Books, 2015.

ACKNOWLEDGEMENTS

Most of all, I owe the appearance of this book to Mr. Hugh Williams of St. Edward's Press. One of my oldest friends, and an enthusiastic supporter of other books of mine that have published recently, in their cases by Ebury Press of the Random House Group, he and I jointly came up with the idea of the unusual project of publishing two new books by me at the same time, and he has been an enthusiastic and helpful supporter in my efforts to put them together. In the "absence" of him, it certainly would not have occurred to me to consider them as possibilities for contacting a publisher about.

Next in importance is my daughter (and partner in our teaching organisation gwynneteaching.com), Miss Chloe Gwynne. She was involved throughout my writing of the book; she constantly made suggestions that I have made use of; and she also undertook the labour of painstakingly reading a late draft and then making further contributions to the text.

I much appreciate, too, the help of Count Nikolai Tolstoy, the author of several books, Miss Gail Foad, Mr. David Kharbanda, and Mrs. Michael (Elizabeth) Spicer, all of whom, in that order chronologically, went through the book carefully and made many useful comments.

I thank them all.

INDEX

Names of the many characters in Shakespeare's plays
that appear only in the lists in chapter 4 of Part I
have not been included in this Index.

235

239

Printed by Printforce, United Kingdom